WHAT'S COOKING
Rice & Risotto

Elizabeth Wolf-Cohen

THUNDER BAY
P·R·E·S·S

First published in the United States in 2000 by
Thunder Bay Press
An imprint of the Advantage Publishers Group
5880 Oberlin Drive, San Diego, CA 92121-4794
www.advantagebooksonline.com

A Parragon book, Parragon, Queen Street House, 4 Queen Street, Bath BA1 1HE, UK

Copyright © Parragon 2000

Library of Congress Cataloging in Publication Data

What's cooking : Rice & risotto.
     p. cm.
    Includes index.
    ISBN 1-57145-254-O
     1. Cookery (Rice) 2, Risotto. 1. Title: What's cooking rice and risotto.
    TX809.R5 W46 2000
    641.6 318--dc21   99-087859

Printed in Indonesia
2 3 4 01 02 03
Produced by Haldane Mason, London

Acknowledgments

Editorial Consultant: Felicity Jackson
Photography: Colin Bowling, Paul Forrester, and Stephen Brayne
Home Economists and Stylist: Mandy Phipps
All props supplied by Barbara Stewart at Surfaces.

North American Edition
Managing Editor: JoAnn Padgett
Project Editor: Elizabeth McNulty

NOTE

Unless otherwise stated, milk is assumed to be full fat,
eggs are medium, and pepper is freshly ground black pepper.

Recipes using uncooked eggs should be
avoided by infants, the elderly, pregnat women, and anyone
suffering from an illness

Contents

Introduction

Rice is the staple food for a third of the world's population and is produced in more than 100 countries. Popular world wide, rice features in the cooking of countries as diverse as China, India, South America, Spain, Portugal, Italy, and Africa. It is important to know about the varieties, so you can choose the appropriate cooking method. Rice surely is the ideal food—easy to store and quick to cook, nutritious and easy to digest, and, above all, delicious.

MAIN RICE VARIETIES

There are many varieties and sub-varieties of rice and different kinds seem to appear on our supermarket shelves every day. The main types are:

Long-grain white rice is milled or polished to remove the outer husk, the germ and most of the bran; the rice has a long shape and a white opaque appearance. Sometimes called Patna rice, because it originally came from that part of India, long-grain rice now comes largely from Thailand and the U.S.A. A popular all-purpose rice in the West for soups, stews, main course dishes, salads, pilafs, accompaniments, and composite dishes, long-grain rice should be light and fluffy with separate grains. Cook for 15–18 minutes by the simmering or absorption method.

Easy-cook rice is parboiled (converted) long-grain white rice. Rice was first parboiled in India as a way of increasing its shelf life and hardness. Parboiling before milling forces the vitamins deeper into the grain, increasing its nutritional value and its cooking time, but only slightly, to 20–25 minutes. Cook by the same methods as long-grain white rice; it is more golden than long-grain white rice.

Long-grain brown rice is a slightly less refined variety that has been milled only to remove the inedible husk. Long-grain brown rice has a distinctly nutty flavor and a much chewier texture. A soft brown color, it is less fluffy than long-grain white rice; it is also available in an easy-cook variety. Brown rice takes slightly longer than white rice to cook, 35–40 minutes, but can be substituted for white rice in most recipes; it is especially good in salads as it has a firmer texture.

Basmati rice is sometimes called the Champagne or king of rice. This long-grain rice grown in India and Pakistan has a distinctive perfume essential in Indian pilafs and biriyanis. It has a very white color and a slimmer grain, and is very light and fluffy when cooked. It can be used as long-grain white rice, but takes less time to cook—10–12 minutes by the simmering or absorption method. Basmati is now available as easy-cook, but takes slightly longer to cook, 18–20 minutes. Brown Basmati Rice is unpolished and only has the husk removed. More nutritious, dense, chewy, and aromatic, it takes a bit longer to cook, 45–50 minutes. Storage time is limited as the natural oils can become rancid.

Italian risotto rice is a superb medium-short-grain Italian rice used almost exclusively for creamy risottos. The rice, grown in Northern Italy, has a visible chalky line down the center. The higher the quality, the more liquid it absorbs; up to three or four times its own volume. When cooked, it forms a creamy soupy sauce with separate grains which maintain a "firm to the bite" texture. Look for arborio, carnaroli, roma, or vialone nano; 18–20 minutes for cooking but generally 25–30 minutes in a risotto.

Spanish calaspara and la bomba rice from the area near Murcia and Valencia are superb quality medium-short-grain rices grown for paella. Substitute Italian risotto rice if you cannot find it. It cooks in about 15–18 minutes, longer in paellas, 30–35 minutes.

Pudding rice or short-grain, sometimes called Carolina rice as it was grown in the southern states of North and South Carolina, is a short-grain or round-grain rice with a chalky appearance and bland flavor. The grains are moist and sticky when cooked—perfect for puddings, custards, desserts, or croquettes. Now mostly exported from China and Australia, 4 tablespoons can thicken 2½ cups of milk.

Thai fragrant rice or jasmine rice is a savory white long-grain rice used in Thai and Southeast Asian cooking. It has a natural aromatic flavor slightly less pronounced than basmati and it is slightly soft and sticky when cooked. Cook as for basmati; with slightly longer cooking time, about 12–15 minutes.

Japanese sushi or sticky rice is an expensive, short-grain, absorbent, sticky rice, perfect for sushi where grains must stick together to hold a shape. The opaque, pearl-like grains are white and round or slightly elongated. Grown in Japan, China, and Thailand, California is now producing a medium-grain version. It cooks in about 15–20 minutes by the absorption method; it is usually mixed with a rice vinegar-sugar seasoning and fanned to cool and create a shiny appearance.

Black sweet rice or black glutinous rice is a medium short-grain rice that has a dark purple-red color. It has a rich flavor that stands up to Asian ingredients such as coconut milk and palm sugar. Used in sweet dishes in Thailand, Vietnam, and Cambodia, it is available in special areas of supermarkets and Asian groceries; it cooks in 25–30 minutes by the absorption method. The color will dye other ingredients and cookware.

Camargue red rice is a medium oval grain with a reddish brown color found in the South of France (Camargue is marshy land in the far southwest). It has an earthy taste and firm chewy texture. Although it loses color in cooking, it looks good and stands up to robust flavors. Longer cooking time of 45–60 minutes by simmering or absorption method is necessary.

Wild rice, not a true rice, but an aquatic grass, is gathered by Native American Indians by canoe. This delicious nutty rice is now being cultivated; expensive, with high-quality long glossy brown-black grains that "flower" when fully cooked. Cook for 55–60 minutes by simmering or absorption or follow the package instructions. As it is very expensive, it is now being sold packaged in combination with long-grain white or basmati rice. It is excellent in soups, salads, stuffings, and pilafs and with full-flavored poultry and sauces.

OTHER RICE PRODUCTS

Ground rice and rice flour is made by milling white rice to a flour-like consistency to be used as a thickener, or in cakes, pastries, cookies, and puddings. Available in varying grades of coarseness from slightly granular to very fine; rice flour is generally the finest.

Rice Flakes are a form of flaked rice used in Far-Eastern cooking styles and generally function as a thickening agent, though can be deep-fat fried as a garnish.

Rice Noodles, including vermicelli, rice sticks, wide rice sticks and others are dry, rice-flour based pasta, twisted into skeins. They range in size from very fine (*sen mee*), to about ⅛ inch thick, like tagliatelle (*sen lek*), to wide, about 1½ inch (*sen yaai*). Rehydrate in hot water for 5–20 minutes, drain, and serve or use in other recipes. Some fresh rice-flour based noodles are available.

Japanese harusame noodles are very thin noodles; treat as rice vermicelli.

Vietnamese rice paper wrappers are used for spring rolls, "wraps" or other dishes. Moistened by dipping briefly into water or spraying, they can be eaten as is, steamed, or fried. They are available in various shapes and sizes.

Rice paper is an edible paper made from rice-like plants. Use it in baking to prevent sticking for foods such as meringues and delicate cookies; very thin and brittle.

Rice vinegars are red, clear, yellow, or black. Wine-based, they are used in salad dressings, dipping sauces, stir-fries, and other rice dishes such as sushi. Flavors range from mellow to rich and fruity. Japanese vinegar is milder than Chinese. Mirin is a Japanese sweetened rice wine. Sake, Japanese rice wine, has a distinctive flavor; sherry can be used as a substitute.

COOKING METHODS

Cooking rice is not difficult, but it is important to choose the right rice for your recipe; the cooking method depends on the type of rice. As a rough guide allow 2 tablespoons of raw brown rice per serving, and ¼ cup for other varieties; pudding recipes will vary. Two of the most basic ways of cooking rice are as follows:

Simmering is the easiest method, but imparts the least flavor. Bring a saucepan of water to a boil. Add a pinch of salt, then sprinkle in the rice and return to a boil. Reduce the heat to medium and simmer for 15–18 minutes for long-grain white rice, 20–25 minutes for easy-cook, and 35–40 minutes for brown rice. Basmati rice takes less cooking time, about 10–12 minutes.

Absorption Method requires the exact amount of liquid that the rice will absorb to be tender. Put the measured rice in a heavy-based saucepan, add a pinch of salt, a tablespoon of oil (optional) and 1½ times the amount of cold water. Bring to a boil over high heat; then reduce the heat to as low as possible and simmer, tightly covered, until the rice is tender and the liquid has been completely absorbed (see simmering method for timings). Do not be tempted to uncover or stir during cooking time; uncovering allows the steam to escape, altering the measured amount of liquid; stirring is even worse—it can break the fragile grains of rice, releasing the starch and making sticky rice.

Remove the pan from the heat and let stand for about 5 minutes; then, using a fork, fluff into a warm serving bowl. Alternatively, after removing from the heat, uncover and place a dish towel or double thickness of paper towel over the rice, re-cover and let stand for 5 minutes. This method allows the steam to be absorbed rather than drip back into the rice, creating a drier, fluffier rice. Many cooks like to put the rice on a "heat-tamer" or heatproof pad to create an even more gentle heat after the rice has come to a boil. If not, you may get a crusty (not burnt) layer of rice stuck to the bottom of the pan. However, in many cultures, this is the best bit—to loosen the crusty layer, place the pan on a wet towel for 5 minutes, then serve, or deep-fry it and serve as a snack!

Pilaf Method In a heavy-based saucepan over medium-high heat, heat two tablespoons of oil or butter and gently cook a finely chopped onion or 2–3 shallots. Add the measured rice and cook, stirring frequently, until the rice is well coated with the fat and is translucent. Add 1½ times stock or water, a pinch of salt, and bring to a boil, stirring once or twice. At this point, cover the surface of the rice with a circle of waxed paper or foil (to prevent the liquid from evaporating too quickly) and cover tightly; reduce the heat to as low as possible. Cooking times are as for the simmering method.

Soups & Salads

Rice not only makes soups and salads more substantial, but also adds an interesting texture and flavor to the dishes.

In the following pages you will find a variety of delicious soups using rice, from the classic Risi e Bisi, flavored with peas, parsley, and Parmesan, to a hearty Chicken & Sausage Gumbo. In Barley & Brown Rice Soup, the rice adds a nutty flavor and creates a deliciously thick consistency, turning it into a warming lunch dish. Pumpkin soup has a deliciously sweet flavor that is subtly enhanced by rice, while in Shrimp Bisque with Rice, rice is used as a thickener without overpowering the delicate flavor of the soup. Soups such as Vietnamese Beef & Rice Noodle Soup feature rice in the form of light, delicate noodles, while a chowder is given a different twist with wild rice and smoked chicken.

In salads, the nutty flavor and chewy texture of wild rice work well with the smoky flavors in Wild Rice & Bacon Salad with Scallops, and add an interesting dimension to a fruity bean salsa. Red rice from the Camargue in the South of France also has a particular nutty flavor, which is good with the spiciness of Red Rice Salad with Hot Dressing.

You can also use rice to give old favorites a lift—try green salad with toasted rice, or turn a Greek salad into a substantial meal by adding cooked rice. Gazpacho Rice Salad is just as refreshing as the classic Spanish soup it is based on, while Caesar Salad is given an exotic touch with Thai flavorings and a rice paper garnish.

Risi e Bisi

This famous Venetian rice soup makes an excellent substantial first course.
It should be thick but not as thick as a risotto.

Serves 4

INGREDIENTS

2 lb. fresh unshelled peas
4 tbsp. unsalted butter
1 onion, finely chopped
3¾ cups chicken stock
1 cup arborio rice

2 tbsp. chopped fresh flat-leaf parsley
⅔ cup freshly grated Parmesan cheese
salt and pepper

TO GARNISH:
tomato slices
Parmesan cheese shavings
fresh basil leaves

1 Remove the peas from their shells—the shelled peas should weigh about 10½ oz.

2 Melt the butter in a large heavy-based saucepan over medium heat. Add the onion and cook for about 2 minutes, stirring occasionally, until beginning to soften.

3 Add the shelled peas and cook, stirring occasionally, for a further 2–3 minutes. Gradually add the chicken stock and bring to a boil. Reduce the heat and simmer, covered, for about 10 minutes, stirring occasionally.

4 Add the rice and season with a little salt and pepper. Simmer, covered, for about 15 minutes, stirring occasionally, until the rice is just tender.

5 Stir in the parsley and adjust the seasoning. If the soup is too thick, add a little more stock. Stir in the Parmesan, then ladle into bowls.

6 Serve immediately, garnished with tomato slices, Parmesan shavings, and basil leaves.

COOK'S TIP

You can substitute 10½ oz. frozen peas for fresh: defrost under running hot water, add to the softened onions, and cook for about 5 minutes with the stock. Continue from Step 4.

Provençal Pumpkin Winter Soup

This sweet-tasting winter soup is found throughout Provence. Sometimes thickened with potatoes or even bread, this soup uses a round rice for extra sweetness and thickening.

Serves 6

INGREDIENTS

2 lb. 4 oz. fresh orange-fleshed
    pumpkin or winter squash, such as
    butternut or hubbard
2 tbsp. olive oil
1 large onion, chopped
2 garlic cloves, chopped
2 tsp. fresh thyme leaves

6¼ cups chicken or vegetable stock, or
    water
1 bay leaf
½ tsp. crushed dried chilies
½ cup short-grain rice, such as
    arborio or valencia
1 tsp. salt

1¼ cups light cream or milk
freshly grated nutmeg
pepper
fresh thyme sprigs, to garnish
garlic croutons, to serve (optional)

1 Remove any seeds from the pumpkin, then peel. Cut into small cubes and set aside.

2 Heat the oil in a large saucepan over medium heat. Add the onion and cook for about 4 minutes until soft.

3 Stir in the garlic and thyme and cook for 1 minute. Stir in the pumpkin, stock, bay leaf, chilies, and half the rice. Bring to a boil, skimming off any foam.

Reduce the heat to low and simmer, covered, for about 1 hour until the pumpkin is very tender.

4 Meanwhile, bring a saucepan of water to a boil. Add the salt, sprinkle in the remaining rice, and simmer for about 15 minutes until tender. Drain, rinse, then drain again. Set aside.

5 Working in batches, process the pumpkin soup in a blender until smooth and strain

into a large saucepan. Add the cooked rice, cream, and nutmeg to taste. Season with salt and pepper and garnish with thyme. Serve with croutons, if desired.

COOK'S TIP

Cooking half the rice separately, then adding it to the pureed soup, gives the finished dish a little texture, but if you prefer a completely smooth soup, cook all the rice at Step 3 and blend.

Tomato & Red Rice Soup

Red rice, with its firm texture and nutty flavor, is particularly good in this soup. However, if you have difficulty in finding it, long-grain brown rice can be used instead very successfully.

Serves 4–6

INGREDIENTS

2 tbsp. olive oil
1 onion, finely chopped
1 carrot, finely chopped
1 stalk celery, finely chopped
3–4 garlic cloves, finely chopped
2 lb. fresh ripe tomatoes, skinned, deseeded, and finely chopped (see Cook's Tip)

1 bay leaf
½ cinnamon stick (optional)
1 tsp. fresh thyme leaves or ½ tsp. dried thyme
1 tsp. dried oregano
1 tbsp. brown sugar
½ tsp. cayenne pepper, or to taste

6¼ cups chicken stock or water
½ cup red rice or long-grain brown rice
1 tbsp. chopped fresh oregano leaves
salt and pepper
freshly grated Parmesan cheese, to serve

1 Heat the oil in a large saucepan over medium heat. Add the onion, carrot, and celery and cook for about 10 minutes, stirring occasionally, until very soft and beginning to color. Stir in the garlic and cook for a further minute.

2 Add the tomatoes, bay leaf, cinnamon stick, if using, thyme, dried oregano, sugar, and cayenne pepper and cook, stirring occasionally, for about 5 minutes until the tomatoes begin to cook down.

3 Add the stock and the rice and bring to a boil, skimming off any foam. Reduce the heat and simmer, covered, for about 30 minutes until the rice is tender, adding more stock if necessary.

4 Stir in the fresh oregano leaves and season with salt and pepper. Serve immediately, with Parmesan cheese for sprinkling.

COOK'S TIP

You need well-flavored tomatoes for this soup; if unavailable, use canned Italian plum tomatoes instead, and reduce the amount of stock if the tomatoes are packed in a lot of juice.

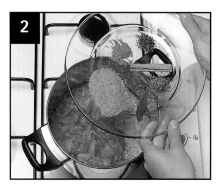

Barley & Rice Soup with Swiss Chard

This hearty winter soup makes a warming lunch or supper when served with a crusty loaf of ciabatta.

Serves 4–6

INGREDIENTS

½ cup pearl barley
½ cup long-grain brown rice
1 lb. Swiss chard, trimmed and soaked
   for 10 minutes
2 tbsp. olive oil
1 large onion, finely chopped
2 carrots, finely chopped
2 stalks celery, finely chopped

2 garlic cloves, finely chopped
14 oz. can chopped Italian plum
   tomatoes with their juice
1 bay leaf
1 tsp. dried thyme
1 tsp. *herbes de Provence* or dried
   oregano
4 cups chicken or vegetable stock

1 lb. can cannellini beans, drained
2 tbsp. chopped fresh parsley
salt and pepper
freshly grated Parmesan cheese, to
   serve

1 Bring a large saucepan of water to a boil. Add the barley and the brown rice and return to a boil. Reduce the heat and simmer gently for 30–35 minutes until just tender. Drain and set aside.

2 Drain the Swiss chard. Cut out the hard white stems and slice the stems crosswise into very thin strips; set aside. Roll the leaves into a long cigar shape and shred thinly; set aside.

3 Heat the oil in a large saucepan. Add the onion, carrots, and celery and cook, stirring frequently, for about 5 minutes until soft and beginning to color. Add the garlic and cook for a minute longer. Add the tomatoes and their juice, the bay leaf, thyme, and *herbes de Provence*. Reduce the heat and simmer, partially covered, for about 7 minutes until all the vegetables are soft.

4 Stir in the sliced white chard stems and the stock. Simmer gently for about 20 minutes. Add the shredded green chard and simmer for a further 15 minutes.

5 Stir in the beans and parsley with the cooked barley and brown rice. Season with salt and pepper. Bring back to a boil and simmer for a further 8-10 minutes. Serve immediately, with Parmesan for sprinkling.

Shrimp Bisque with Rice

*A bisque is a shellfish soup enriched with cream and, because of the delicate flavors,
it is traditionally thickened with rice. Using basmati rice adds a slightly exotic scent.*

Serves 6

INGREDIENTS

1 lb. 6 oz. cooked shrimp, in their shell

1 stalk celery, with leaves if possible, chopped

$1/2$ tsp. crushed dried chilies

about 5 cups water

4 tbsp. butter

1 onion, finely chopped

2 carrots, finely chopped

$1/4$ cup brandy or cognac

1 cup dry white wine

1 bay leaf and 10 parsley sprigs, tied together with kitchen string

1–2 tsp. tomato paste

1 tsp. paprika

3 tbsp. basmati or long-grain white rice

$2/3$ cup heavy or whipping cream

fresh dill sprigs or long chives, to garnish

1. Peel 6 shrimp, leaving the tails intact; reserve these shrimp for garnishing the bisque. Peel the remaining shrimp, reserving the shells.

2. Put all the shells in a saucepan, with the celery stalk and dried chilies. Add the water. Bring to a boil over high heat, skimming off any foam. Reduce the heat and simmer gently for about 30 minutes. Strain and set aside.

3. Melt the butter in a large saucepan. Add the onion and carrots and cook for about 8 minutes, stirring frequently, until the vegetables are soft. Add the brandy and, standing well back, ignite with a long match. Allow the flames to die down, then stir in the wine. Boil for about 5 minutes to reduce by about half.

4. Add the reserved stock, bay leaf and parsley stem bundle, tomato paste, paprika, and rice; stir. Bring to a boil, then simmer gently for 20 minutes until the rice is very tender.

5. Remove the parsley bundle. Working in batches if necessary, process the soup in a blender and strain into a clean saucepan. Stir in the cream and simmer for 2–3 minutes. Add the 6 shrimp and heat through for a minute. Ladle into 6 bowls, arranging a shrimp in each serving. Garnish and serve.

Italian Endive & Rice Soup

This is a simple Italian soup made with the slightly bitter green scarola, or escarole, a member of the chicory family. The rice thickens the soup and gives it a delicate creaminess.

Serves 4–6

INGREDIENTS

1 lb. (about 7 heads) endive
4 tbsp. butter
1 onion, finely chopped
4 cups chicken stock

½ cup arborio or carnaroli rice
freshly grated nutmeg
2–4 tbsp. freshly grated Parmesan
   cheese

salt and pepper
fresh herbs, to garnish

1 Separate the leaves from the endive, discarding any damaged outer leaves. Wash the leaves thoroughly under cold running water and drain well. Stack several leaves in a pile and roll tightly, then shred the leaves into 1½-inch ribbons and set aside. Continue with the remaining leaves.

2 Melt the butter in a large heavy-based saucepan over medium heat. Add the onion and cook, stirring occasionally, for about 4 minutes until soft and just beginning to color. Stir in the shredded endive and cook, stirring frequently, for 2 minutes until the leaves wilt.

3 Add half the stock and season with salt and pepper. Reduce the heat and simmer, covered, over very low heat for 25–35 minutes until tender.

4 Add the remaining stock, and bring to a boil. Sprinkle in the rice and simmer, partially covered, over medium heat for 15–20 minutes, stirring occasionally, until the rice is just tender, yet firm to the bite.

5 Remove from the heat and season with more salt and pepper, if necessary, and nutmeg. Ladle into bowls and sprinkle with a little Parmesan. Serve immediately, garnished with herbs.

COOK'S TIP

Long-grain white rice can be substituted for arborio or carnaroli, but the round rice is slightly more starchy.

Turkey & Rice Soup

You can always use the leftover turkey from Christmas or Thanksgiving to make the stock for this rich and satisfying soup.

Serves 8–10

INGREDIENTS

1 onion, finely chopped
2 carrots, diced
1 cup long-grain white rice
2 leeks, thinly sliced
1½ cups frozen peas
4 oz. fresh or frozen (defrosted)
   snow peas, thinly sliced
115 g/4 oz. fresh spinach or
   watercress, washed and shredded

1 lb. cooked turkey meat, diced
1 tbsp. finely chopped fresh parsley
salt and pepper

STOCK:
1 bunch fresh parsley
2 turkey legs
1 bay leaf
1 tsp. dried thyme

2 onions, unpeeled, cut into quarters
2 carrots, cut into chunks
2 stalks celery, cut into chunks
1 parsnip, cut into chunks (optional)
1 dessert apple or pear (optional)
1 tbsp. black peppercorns

1 To make the stock, first tie the parsley sprigs into a bundle, then put in a large pan with the remaining stock ingredients and enough cold water to cover by 1 inch.

2 Bring to a boil, over high heat, skimming off any foam. Boil for 2 minutes, then reduce the heat to low and simmer very gently for 2–3 hours. Cool the stock slightly, then strain into a large bowl. Skim off any fat from the surface, then wipe a paper towel across the surface.

3 Put about 12 cups of the turkey stock in a large saucepan. Add the onion and carrots and bring to a boil.

4 Add the rice, reduce the heat, and simmer for 15–20 minutes until the rice is tender, stirring once or twice.

5 Stir the remaining vegetables into the pan of soup and simmer for 10 minutes. Add the cooked turkey meat, heat through, and season with salt and pepper. Stir in the parsley and serve.

Wild Rice & Smoked Chicken Chowder

Adding wild rice to soups gives wonderful texture as well as flavor—and it looks good, too.
The smoky flavor of the chicken complements the nuttiness of the wild rice.

Serves 6–8

INGREDIENTS

½ cup wild rice, washed

3 fresh ears of corn on the cob, husks
    and silks removed

2 tbsp. vegetable oil

1 large onion, finely chopped

1 stalk celery, thinly sliced

1 leek, trimmed and thinly sliced

½ tsp. dried thyme

2 tbsp. all-purpose flour

14 cups chicken stock

9 oz. boned smoked chicken, skinned,
    diced, or shredded

1 cup heavy or whipping cream

1 tbsp. chopped fresh dill

salt and pepper

fresh dill sprigs, to garnish

1 Bring a large saucepan of water to a boil. Add a tablespoon of salt and sprinkle in the wild rice. Return to a boil, then reduce the heat and simmer, covered, for about 40 minutes until just tender, but still firm to the bite. Do not overcook the rice as it will continue to cook in the soup. Drain and rinse; set aside.

2 Hold the corn cobs vertical to a cutting board and, using a sharp heavy knife, cut down along the cobs to remove the kernels.

Set aside the kernels. Scrape the cob to remove the milky juices; reserve for the soup.

3 Heat the oil in a large pan over medium heat. Add the onion, celery, leek, and dried thyme. Cook, stirring frequently, for about 8 minutes until the vegetables are very soft.

4 Sprinkle othe flour over and stir until blended. Gradually whisk in the stock, add the corn with any juices, and bring to a boil;

skim off any foam. Reduce the heat and simmer for about 25 minutes until the vegetables are very soft and tender.

5 Stir in the smoked chicken, wild rice, cream, and dill. Season with salt and pepper. Simmer for 10 minutes until the chicken and rice are heated through. Garnish with dill sprigs and serve immediately.

Chicken & Sausage Gumbo

This is the nearest you can get to a true gumbo living outside "Cajun country."
Gumbos are always served around a dome of white rice.

Serves 6–8

INGREDIENTS

2 lb. 12 oz. chicken, cut into
  8 pieces
¾ cup all-purpose flour
¾ cup vegetable oil
1 lb. 9 oz. andouille (Cajun smoked
  sausage), Polish kielbasa,
  or other smoked pork sausage,
  cut into 2-inch pieces
2 large onions, finely chopped

3–4 stalks celery, finely chopped
2 green bell peppers, deseeded and
  finely chopped
1 lb. 9 oz. okra, stems trimmed and cut
  into ½-inch pieces
4 garlic cloves, finely chopped
2 bay leaves
½ tsp. cayenne pepper, or to taste
1 tsp. ground black pepper
1 tsp. any dry mustard powder

1 tsp. dried thyme
½ tsp. ground cumin
½ tsp. dried oregano
6¼ cups chicken stock, simmering
3–4 ripe tomatoes, deseeded and
  chopped
salt
2 cups long-grain white rice, cooked,
  to serve

1 Toss the chicken in about 2 tablespoons of the flour. Heat 2 tablespoons of the oil in a large skillet. Add the chicken and cook for about 10 minutes until golden. Set aside.

2 Add the sausage pieces to the pan, stirring and tossing, for about 5 minutes until beginning to color. Set aside.

3 Heat the remaining oil in the cleaned-out pan until just beginning to smoke. Add the remaining flour all at once and whisk immediately to blend into the oil. Reduce the heat and cook, stirring, for about 20 minutes until the roux is a deep rich brown.

4 Add the onions, celery, and bell peppers to the roux and cook, stirring frequently, for about 3 minutes until beginning to soften. Stir in the okra, garlic, bay leaves, cayenne pepper, black pepper, mustard powder, thyme, cumin, and oregano and stir well.

5 Little by little, whisk the hot stock into the mixture, stirring well after each addition. Simmer for about 10 minutes. Stir in the tomatoes and the reserved sausage and chicken pieces and simmer for about 20 minutes until the meat is tender.

6 To serve, fill a cup with rice, packing it lightly, then unmold into the center of a wide soup bowl. Spoon the gumbo around the rice.

Vietnamese Beef & Rice Noodle Soup

Exotic flavors combine with French finesse in this exquisitely delicious main course soup, called "pho" in Vietnam. If you can, make the stock a day in advance for the best flavor.

Serves 4–6

INGREDIENTS

6 oz. package dried rice stick noodles

4–6 scallions, sliced thinly on the diagonal

1 fresh red chili, sliced thinly on the diagonal

1 bunch fresh cilantro

1 bunch fresh mint

12 oz. fillet or stalk eye steak, very thinly sliced

salt and pepper

STOCK:

2 lb. meaty beef bones

4 scallions, chopped

2 carrots, cut into chunks

1 leek, cut into chunks

3 whole star anise

1 tsp. black peppercorns

1 To make the stock, put the beef bones, scallions, carrots, leek, star anise, and peppercorns in a large saucepan or flameproof casserole and bring to a boil, skimming off any foam. Reduce the heat and simmer gently, partially covered, for about 3 hours.

2 Strain into a large bowl and skim off any fat; draw a paper towel across the surface to remove any drops of fat.

3 Cover the noodles with warm water and let them stand for about 3 minutes until just softened; drain the noodles. Using scissors, snip the noodles into 4-inch lengths.

4 Arrange the scallions and chili on a serving plate. Strip the leaves from the cilantro stems and arrange in a pile on the plate. Strip the leaves from the mint stems and arrange in a pile next to the cilantro leaves.

5 Bring the beef stock to a boil in a large saucepan. Add the noodles and simmer for about 2 minutes until tender. Add the beef strips and simmer for about 1 minute. Season to taste.

6 Ladle the soup into bowls and serve with the scallions, chili, and herbs passed separately.

Warm Greek-style Rice Salad

This easy-to-make rice salad has all the flavors of the Aegean—olive oil, lemon, feta cheese, capers, and tomatoes. It is ideal as an accompaniment to barbecued lamb or chicken.

Serves 4–6

INGREDIENTS

1 cup long-grain white rice
$\frac{1}{3}$ cup extra-virgin olive oil
2–3 tbsp. lemon juice
1 tbsp. chopped fresh oregano or 1 tsp. dried oregano
$\frac{1}{2}$ tsp. Dijon mustard

2 large ripe tomatoes, deseeded and chopped
1 red or green bell pepper, deseeded and chopped
$2\frac{3}{4}$ oz. Kalamata or other brine-cured black olives, pitted and halved

8 oz. feta cheese, crumbled, plus extra cubes, to garnish
1 tbsp. capers, rinsed and drained
2–4 tbsp. chopped fresh flat-leaf parsley or cilantro
salt and pepper
diced cucumber, to garnish

1 Bring a saucepan of water to a boil. Add a teaspoon of salt and sprinkle in the rice; return to a boil, stirring once or twice. Reduce the heat and simmer for 15–20 minutes until the rice is tender, stirring once or twice. Drain and rinse under hot running water; drain again.

2 Meanwhile, whisk together the olive oil, lemon juice, oregano, mustard, and salt and pepper in a bowl. Add the tomatoes, bell pepper, olives, feta cheese, capers, and parsley and stir to coat in the dressing. Marinate.

3 Turn the rice into a large bowl; add to the vegetable mixture and toss to mix well.

4 Season the salad with salt and pepper to taste, then divide between 4–6 individual dishes and garnish with extra feta cheese cubes and diced cucumber. Serve just warm.

VARIATION

This salad is also delicious made with brown rice—just increase the cooking time to 25–30 minutes.

Wild Rice & Bacon Salad with Scallops

*Wild rice has a nutty, slightly chewy texture that is great in salads.
The smokiness of the bacon and the sweetness of the scallops make a perfect combination.*

Serves 4

INGREDIENTS

1 cup wild rice
2¹/₂ cups water or more if necessary
¹/₂ cup pecans or walnuts
2 tbsp. vegetable oil
4 slices smoked bacon, diced or sliced

3–4 shallots, finely chopped
¹/₃ cup walnut oil
2–3 tbsp. sherry or cider vinegar
2 tbsp. chopped fresh dill

8–12 large scallops, cut lengthwise
  in half
salt and pepper
lemon and lime slices, to serve

1 Put the wild rice in a saucepan with the water and bring to a boil, stirring once or twice. Reduce the heat to low, cover, and simmer gently for 30–50 minutes, depending on whether you prefer a chewy or tender texture. Using a fork, fluff the rice into a large bowl; allow to cool slightly.

2 Meanwhile, toast the nuts in a skillet for 2–3 minutes until just beginning to color, stirring frequently. Cool and chop coarsely; set aside.

3 Heat a tablespoon of the vegetable oil in the pan. Stir in the bacon and cook, stirring occasionally, until crisp and brown. Transfer to paper towels to drain. Remove some of the oil from the pan and stir in the shallots. Cook for 3–4 minutes, stirring from time to time, until soft.

4 Stir the toasted nuts, bacon, and shallots into the rice. Add the walnut oil, vinegar, half the chopped dill, and salt and pepper to taste. Toss well to combine the ingredients, then set aside.

5 Brush a large non-stick skillet with the remaining oil. Heat until very hot, add the scallops, and cook for 1 minute on each side until golden; do not overcook.

6 Divide the wild rice salad among 4 individual plates. Top with the scallops and sprinkle with the remaining dill. Garnish with a sprig of dill, if desired, and serve immediately with the lemon and lime slices.

Spicy Rice, Bean, & Corn Salad

This hearty rice salad was inspired by the famous American dish called succotash. It is easy to put together and makes a great addition to a summer barbecue or broiled chicken or pork.

Serves 4–6

INGREDIENTS

½ cup long-grain white or brown rice
3 ears of corn on the cob
peanut oil
1 small red onion, finely chopped

1 fresh red or green chili, deseeded and finely chopped
1 tbsp. lemon juice
1 tbsp. lime juice
½ tsp. cayenne pepper, or to taste

2 tbsp. chopped fresh cilantro
14 oz. can butter beans
4 oz. sliced cooked ham, diced
salt and pepper

1 Bring a saucepan of water to a boil. Add a teaspoon of salt and sprinkle in the rice. Return to a boil, stirring once or twice. Reduce the heat and simmer for 15–20 minutes until the rice is tender. (Brown rice will take 25–30 minutes.) Drain and rinse under cold running water; drain and set aside.

2 Scrape down each corn cob with a knife to remove the kernels; set aside. Scrape along each cob to remove the milky residue and transfer to a small bowl.

3 Heat 1 tablespoon of the oil in a saucepan. Add the corn kernels and cook gently for about 5 minutes, stirring frequently, until tender. Add the red onion and chili and stir for about 1 minute until blended. Transfer to a plate and allow to cool slightly.

4 Place the lemon and lime juices in a large bowl and whisk in the cayenne pepper, 2–3 tablespoons of oil, and the milky corn liquid. Whisk in the chopped cilantro until well combined.

5 Using a fork, fluff in the cooked rice and corn and onion mixture. Add the beans and ham and season with salt and pepper. Transfer to a serving bowl and serve immediately.

COOK'S TIP

Although fresh corn on the cob has a delicious flavor, you could substitute canned or defrosted frozen corn kernels without any problem.

Gazpacho Rice Salad

This rice salad has all the flavors of a zesty Spanish gazpacho. Garlic, tomatoes, bell peppers, and cucumber combined with rice make a great summer salad.

Serves 4–6

INGREDIENTS

extra-virgin olive oil
1 onion, finely chopped
4 garlic cloves, finely chopped
1 cup long-grain white rice or basmati
1 1/2 cups vegetable stock or water
1 1/2 tsp. dried thyme
3 tbsp. sherry vinegar
1 tsp. Dijon mustard
1 tsp. honey or sugar

1 red bell pepper, cored, deseeded, and chopped
1/2 yellow bell pepper, cored, deseeded, and chopped
1/2 green bell pepper, cored, deseeded, and chopped
1 red onion, finely chopped
1/2 cucumber, peeled, deseeded, and chopped (optional)

3 tomatoes, deseeded and chopped
2–3 tbsp. chopped flat-leaf parsley
salt and pepper

TO SERVE:
12 cherry tomatoes, halved
12 black olives, pitted and coarsely chopped
1 tbsp. slivered almonds, toasted

1 Heat 2 tablespoons of the oil in a large saucepan. Add the onion and cook for 2 minutes, stirring frequently, until beginning to soften. Stir in half the garlic and cook for a further minute.

2 Add the rice, stirring well to coat, and cook for about 2 minutes until translucent. Stir in the stock and half the thyme and bring to a boil; season with salt and pepper. Simmer very gently, covered, for about 20 minutes until tender. Stand, still covered, for about 15 minutes; uncover and cool completely.

3 Whisk the vinegar with the remaining garlic and thyme, the mustard, honey, and salt and pepper in a large bowl. Slowly whisk in about 1/3 cup of the olive oil. Using a fork, fluff the rice into the vinaigrette.

4 Add the bell peppers, red onion, cucumber, tomatoes, and parsley; toss and season.

5 Transfer to a serving bowl and garnish with the tomatoes, olives, and almonds. Serve warm.

Thai-style Caesar Salad

This simple salad uses fried rice paper wrappers as crispy croutons on a simple salad of romaine leaves. The Thai fish sauce gives the dressing an unusual flavor.

Serves 4

INGREDIENTS

1 large head romaine lettuce, with
   outer leaves removed, or 2 hearts
vegetable oil, for deep frying
4–6 large rice paper wrappers or
   4 oz. rice paper flakes

small bunch of cilantro, leaves
   stripped from stems

DRESSING:
⅓ cup rice vinegar
2–3 tbsp. Thai fish sauce

2 garlic cloves, coarsely chopped
1 tbsp. sugar
1-inch piece fresh ginger root, peeled
   and coarsely chopped
½ cup sunflower oil
salt and pepper

1 Tear the lettuce leaves into bite-sized pieces and put into a large salad bowl.

2 To make the dressing, put the vinegar, fish sauce, garlic, sugar, and ginger in a food processor and process for 15–30 seconds.

3 With the machine running, gradually pour in the sunflower oil until a creamy liquid forms. Season with salt and pepper and pour into a jug; set aside.

4 Heat about 3 inches of vegetable oil in a deep-fat fryer to 375°F.

5 Meanwhile, break the rice wrappers into bite-sized pieces and dip each into a bowl of water to soften. Lay on a clean dish towel and pat completely dry.

6 Working in batches, add the rice paper pieces to the hot oil and fry for about 15 seconds until crisp and golden. Using a slotted spoon, transfer to paper towels to drain.

7 Add the cilantro leaves to the lettuce and toss to mix. Add the fried rice paper "chips" and drizzle the dressing over. Toss to coat the leaves and serve immediately.

VARIATION

Substitute 2 tablespoons of the sunflower oil with sesame oil for a different flavor.

Brown Rice, Lentil, & Shiitake Salad

Fresh shiitakes, which are now widely available,
give this substantial salad a good mushroomy flavor.

Serves 6–8

INGREDIENTS

1 cup Puy lentils, rinsed
4 tbsp. olive oil
1 onion, finely chopped
1 cup long-grain brown rice
$\frac{1}{2}$ tsp. dried thyme
2 cups chicken stock
12 oz. shiitake mushrooms, trimmed
  and sliced
2 garlic cloves, finely chopped

4 oz. smoked bacon, diced and fried
  until crisp
2 small zucchini, diced
1–2 stalks celery, thinly sliced
6 scallions, thinly sliced
2–3 tbsp. chopped fresh flat-leaf parsley
2 tbsp. walnut halves, toasted and
  coarsely chopped
salt and pepper

DRESSING:
2 tbsp. red or white wine vinegar
1 tbsp. balsamic vinegar
1 tsp. Dijon mustard
1 tsp. sugar
$\frac{1}{3}$ cup extra-virgin olive oil
2–3 tbsp. walnut oil

1 Bring a large saucepan of water to a boil. Add the lentils, bring back to a boil, then simmer for about 30 minutes until just tender; do not overcook. Drain and rinse under cold running water; drain and set aside.

2 Heat 2 tablespoons of the oil in a large saucepan. Add the onion and cook until it begins to soften. Add the rice; stir to coat.

Add the thyme, stock, and salt and pepper; bring to a boil. Simmer very gently, covered tightly, for about 40 minutes until the rice is tender and the liquid absorbed.

3 Heat the remaining oil in a skillet and stir-fry the mushrooms for about 5 minutes until golden. Stir in the garlic and cook for a further 30 seconds. Season with salt and pepper.

4 To make the dressing, whisk together the vinegars, mustard, and sugar in a large bowl. Gradually whisk in the oils. Season with salt and pepper. Add the lentils and gently toss. Fork in the rice. Toss.

5 Stir in the bacon and mushrooms, then zucchini, celery, scallions, and parsley, and season. Serve sprinkled with walnuts.

Moroccan Mixed Rice Salad

The combination of spices gives this rice salad a slightly exotic scent. Toasting the spices mellows the harshness and brings out their flavors.

Serves 4–6

INGREDIENTS

3¹/₂ cups water
1 tbsp. soy sauce
1 tbsp. unsulphured molasses
¹/₂ cup wild rice
2 tbsp. olive oil
¹/₂ cup long-grain brown or white rice
15 oz. can chickpeas, rinsed and drained
¹/₂ red onion, finely chopped

1 small red bell pepper, deseeded and diced
3 oz. ready-soaked dried apricots, sliced
¹/₂ cup raisins
2 tbsp. chopped fresh mint or cilantro
scant ¹/₂ cup slivered almonds, toasted
lettuce leaves, to garnish
lemon wedges, to serve

SPICED DRESSING:
1 tsp. hot curry powder
1 tsp. ground coriander
1 tsp. ground turmeric
1 tsp. freshly ground nutmeg
¹/₂ tsp. cayenne pepper
¹/₄ cup rice vinegar
2 tbsp. honey
1 tbsp. lemon juice
¹/₃ cup extra-virgin olive oil

1 Put 1½ cups of the water, the soy sauce and molasses in a saucepan and bring to a boil. Add the wild rice and bring back to a boil. Cover and simmer gently for 30–50 minutes, depending on whether you prefer a chewy or tender texture. Remove from the heat to cool slightly.

2 Heat the oil in a saucepan, add the brown rice, and stir for about 2 minutes to coat with the oil. Add the remaining water and bring to a boil; reduce the heat to low and simmer, covered tightly, for about 40 minutes until the rice is tender and all the water is absorbed. Remove from the heat to cool slightly.

3 Meanwhile, make the dressing; put the ground spices in a small skillet and cook gently for 4–5 minutes, stirring, until golden. Cool on a small plate. Whisk together the vinegar, honey, and lemon juice in a large bowl, then whisk in the oil, until the dressing thickens. Whisk in the cooled spice mixture.

4 Fork the brown rice and wild rice into the dressing and mix well. Stir in the chickpeas, onion, bell pepper, apricots, raisins, and mint.

5 To serve, sprinkle with the almonds, garnish with lettuce, and serve with lemon wedges.

Pesto Risotto-rice Salad

This is a cross between a risotto and a rice salad—using Italian arborio rice produces a slightly heavier, stickier result. Substituting long-grain white rice will make a lighter fluffier salad.

Serves 4–6

INGREDIENTS

extra-virgin olive oil
1 onion, finely chopped
1 cup arborio rice
2 cups boiling water
6 sun-dried tomatoes, cut into thin
    slivers
1/2 small red onion, very thinly sliced
3 tbsp. lemon juice

PESTO:
2 oz. lightly packed fresh basil leaves
2 garlic cloves, finely chopped
2 tbsp. pine nuts, lightly toasted
1/2 cup extra-virgin olive oil
1/2 cup freshly grated Parmesan cheese
salt and pepper

TO GARNISH:
fresh basil leaves
Parmesan shavings

1 To make the pesto, put the basil, garlic, and pine nuts in a food processor and process for about 30 seconds. With the machine running, gradually pour in the olive oil through the feed tube, until a smooth paste forms. Add the cheese and pulse several times, until blended but still with some texture. Scrape the pesto into a small bowl and season with salt and pepper to taste. Set aside.

2 Heat 1 tablespoon of the oil in a saucepan. Add the onion and cook until beginning to soften. Add the rice and stir to coat. Cook, stirring occasionally, for about 2 minutes. Stir in a boiling water and salt and pepper. Cover and simmer very gently for 20 minutes until the rice is just tender and the water absorbed. Cool slightly.

3 Put the sun-dried tomatoes and sliced onion in a large bowl, add the lemon juice and about 2 tablespoons of oil. Fork in the hot rice and stir in the pesto. Toss to combine. Adjust the seasoning if necessary. Cover and cool to room temperature.

4 Fork the rice mixture into a shallow serving bowl. Drizzle with some olive oil and garnish with basil leaves and Parmesan. Serve the salad at room temperature, not chilled.

Red Rice Salad with Hot Dressing

*This hearty salad is made with red rice from the Camargue in the South of France.
It has an earthy flavor, which goes well with the other robust ingredients.*

Serves 6–8

INGREDIENTS

1 tbsp. olive oil
1 cup red rice
2¹/₂ cups water
14 oz. can red kidney beans, rinsed
   and drained
1 small red bell pepper, cored,
   deseeded, and diced

1 small red onion, finely chopped
2 small cooked beets (not in vinegar),
   peeled and diced
6–8 red radishes, thinly sliced
2–3 tbsp. chopped fresh chives
salt and pepper
fresh chives, to garnish

HOT DRESSING:
2 tbsp. prepared horseradish
1 tbsp. Dijon mustard
1 tsp. sugar
¹/₄ cup red wine vinegar
¹/₂ cup extra-virgin olive oil

1 Put the olive oil and red rice in a heavy-based saucepan and place over medium heat. Add the water and 1 teaspoon of salt. Bring to a boil, reduce the heat and simmer, covered, until the rice is tender and all the water is absorbed (see Cook's Tip). Remove from the heat and allow the rice to cool to room temperature.

2 To make the dressing, put the horseradish, mustard, and sugar in a small bowl and whisk to combine. Whisk in the vinegar, then gradually whisk in the oil to form a smooth dressing.

3 In a large bowl, combine the red kidney beans, red bell pepper, red onion, beets, radishes, and chives and toss together. Season with salt and pepper.

4 Using a fork, fluff the rice into the bowl with the vegetables and toss together. Pour the dressing over and toss well. Cover and let the salad stand for about 1 hour. Spoon into a large shallow serving bowl, garnish with fresh chives, and serve immediately.

COOK'S TIP

There are several red rice varieties on the market. Read the labels carefully, as some require longer cooking than others.

Fruity Wild Rice Salsa with Black Beans

Wild rice has a nutty flavor and a good texture, ideal for salsas and salads. Black beans are popular in Latin-American cooking and can stand up to the strong flavors in salsas.

Serves 4–6

INGREDIENTS

1 cup small black beans, soaked overnight in cold water
1 onion, studded with 4 cloves
1 cup wild rice
2 garlic cloves, trimmed
2 cups boiling water
1 red onion, finely chopped
2 fresh red chilies, deseeded and thinly sliced

1 large red bell pepper, deseeded and chopped
1 small mango or papaya, peeled and diced
2 oranges, segments removed and juice reserved
4 passion fruits, pulp and juice
juice of 3–4 limes
1/2 tsp. ground cumin

1 tbsp. maple syrup or light brown sugar
2/3 cup extra-virgin olive oil
1 small bunch cilantro, leaves stripped from stems and chopped
lime slices, to garnish

1 Drain the soaked beans and put in a large saucepan with the clove-studded onion. Cover with cold water by at least 2 inches. Bring to a boil, reduce the heat to low, and simmer for 1 hour until the beans are tender. Discard the onion, rinse under cold running water, drain and set aside.

2 Meanwhile, put the wild rice and garlic in a saucepan and cover with a boiling water. Simmer, covered, over low heat for 30–50 minutes depending on the preferred texture. Cool slightly; discard the garlic cloves.

3 Put the beans in a large bowl and fork in the wild rice. Add the onion, chilies, bell pepper, mango, orange segments and their juice, and the passion fruit pulp and juice. Toss well together.

4 Combine the lime juice, ground cumin, and maple syrup. Whisk in the olive oil and half the cilantro, then pour over the bean/rice mixture and toss well. Cover and allow the flavors to blend for up to 2 hours.

5 Spoon into a serving bowl, sprinkle with the remaining cilantro, and serve, garnished with lime slices.

Shrimp Salad & Toasted Rice

*This simple salad is tossed with an unusual Vietnamese-style dressing
and sprinkled with dry toasted rice, which gives interesting texture and flavor.*

Serves 4

INGREDIENTS

8 oz. raw cooked shrimp, with tail
    shells left on
2 tbsp. sunflower oil
cayenne pepper
1 tbsp. long-grain white rice
1 large head romaine lettuce with
    outer leaves removed, or 2 hearts

½ small English cucumber, lightly
    peeled, deseeded, and thinly sliced
1 small bunch chives, sliced into
    1-inch pieces
handful of fresh mint leaves
salt and pepper

DRESSING:
¼ cup rice vinegar
1 red chili, deseeded and thinly sliced
3-inch piece lemon grass stalk, crushed
juice of 1 lime
2 tbsp. Thai fish sauce
1 tsp. sugar, or to taste

1 Split each shrimp in half lengthwise, leaving the tail attached to one half. Remove any dark intestinal veins and pat dry. Sprinkle with a little salt and cayenne pepper.

2 To make the dressing, combine the vinegar with the chili and lemon grass. Marinate.

3 Heat a wok or heavy-based skillet over high heat. Add the rice and stir until brown and richly fragrant. Pour into a mortar and cool completely. Crush gently with a pestle until coarse crumbs form.

4 Stir-fry the shrimp in the cleaned pan for 1 minute until warm. Transfer to a plate and season with pepper.

5 Tear or shred the lettuce into large bite-sized pieces and transfer to a shallow salad bowl. Add the cucumber, chives, and mint leaves and toss to combine.

6 Remove the lemon grass and most of the chili slices from the rice vinegar and whisk in the lime juice, fish sauce, water, and sugar. Pour most of the dressing over the salad and toss. Top with the shrimp and drizzle with the remaining dressing. Sprinkle with the toasted rice and serve.

Thai Noodle Salad with Shrimp

This delicious combination of rice noodles and shrimp, lightly dressed with typical Thai flavors, makes an impressive first course or light lunch.

Serves 4

INGREDIENTS

3 oz. rice vermicelli or rice sticks

6 oz. snow peas, cut crosswise in half, if large

5 tbsp. lime juice

4 tbsp. Thai fish sauce

1 tbsp. sugar, or to taste

1-inch piece fresh ginger root, peeled and finely chopped

1 fresh red chili, deseeded and thinly sliced on the diagonal

4 tbsp. chopped fresh cilantro or mint, plus extra for garnishing

4-inch piece of cucumber, peeled, deseeded and diced

2 scallions, thinly sliced on the diagonal

16–20 large cooked, peeled shrimp

2 tbsp. chopped unsalted peanuts or cashews (optional)

4 whole cooked shrimp and lemon slices, to garnish

1 Put the rice noodles in a large bowl and pour enough hot water over to cover. Let stand for about 4 minutes until soft. Drain and rinse under cold running water; drain and set aside.

2 Bring a saucepan of water to a boil. Add the snow peas and return to a boil. Simmer for 1 minute. Drain, rinse under cold running water until cold, then drain and set aside.

3 In a large bowl, whisk together the lime juice, fish sauce, sugar, ginger, chili, and cilantro. Stir in the cucumber and scallions. Add the drained noodles, snow peas, and the shrimp. Toss the salad gently together.

4 Divide the noodle salad among 4 large plates. Sprinkle with chopped cilantro and the peanuts (if using), then garnish each plate with a whole shrimp

and a lemon slice. Serve immediately.

COOK'S TIP

There are many sizes of rice noodles available. Make sure you use the very thin rice noodles, called rice vermicelli or rice sticks or sen mee—otherwise the salad will be too heavy.

Wild Rice Blini with Smoked Salmon

Blinis are small Russian pancakes made with a combination of white and buckwheat flours.
The addition of wild rice adds more texture and a nutty flavor to a real classic.

Makes about 50 blinis

INGREDIENTS

butter or oil for frying
4 scallions, thinly sliced on the
   diagonal
4 oz. smoked salmon, thinly sliced or
   shredded
½ cup sour cream
chopped chives, to garnish

BLINIS:
⅓ cup lukewarm water
1½ tsp. dried yeast
½ cup all-purpose flour
½ cup plus 1 tbsp. buckwheat flour
2 tbsp. sugar
½ tsp. salt

1 cup milk
2 eggs, separated
2 tbsp. butter, melted
1 cup cooked wild rice

1. Pour the lukewarm water into a small bowl and sprinkle the yeast over. Let stand until the yeast has dissolved and the mixture is beginning to bubble.

2. Sift the flours into a large bowl and stir in the sugar and salt. Make a well in the center. Warm ¾ cup milk and add to the well with the yeast mixture. Gradually whisk the flour into the liquid to form a smooth batter.

Cover the bowl with plastic wrap and let stand in a warm place until light and bubbly.

3. Beat the remaining milk with the egg yolks and the melted butter and beat into the batter.

4. Using an electric mixer, beat the egg whites until soft peaks form. Fold a spoonful into the batter, then fold in the remaining egg whites and the wild rice alternately; do not overmix.

5. Heat a little butter or oil in a large skillet to lightly coat. Drop tablespoons of the batter into the pan and cook for 1–2 minutes until tiny bubbles form on the surface. Turn and cook for 30 seconds. Remove and keep warm in a low oven while cooking the remaining batter.

6. To serve, top with the scallions, smoked salmon strips, a dollop of sour cream, and a sprinkling of chives.

Main Dishes & Accompaniments

Rice, like wheat, is one of the world's most versatile ingredients. It can be used as the focal point of a main dish or as a subtle accompaniment to roasts and stews.

Use rice as the base of a substantial dish like Chicken Basquaise, to soak up the flavors of South West France, or combine it with lamb and exotic spices to create a delicious Eastern-style pilaf, perfect for informal entertaining. Rice is ideal for making one-pot dishes—Seafood Rice, a marvelous mix of mussels, clams, peppers, and chili, proves the point—or follow the Cuban tradition of serving rice with black beans, sausage, and ham for a truly satisfying dish.

Try transforming rice into curried patties, a tasty vegetarian alternative to burgers, or use rice as a foil to the strong flavors of stir-fries—the ginger fried rice dish, topped with succulent soy-glazed duck, is an Asian treat. Noodles made from rice also provide excellent all-in-one dishes— try Pad Thai with chicken and crab for an exotic supper.

Delicate flavors go well with rice, especially if the rice is used as an accompaniment. Lemon-scented Rice with Mint will enhance any dish, from a Middle-Eastern tajine to a French beef casserole, while Fragrant Orange Basmati Rice is the perfect accompaniment to steamed fish or poultry dishes.

Chicken Basquaise

Sweet bell peppers are a typical ingredient of dishes from the Basque region in the far West of France. In this recipe, the addition of Bayonne ham, the famous air-dried ham from the Pyrenees, adds a delicious flavor.

Serves 4–5

INGREDIENTS

3 lb. chicken, cut into 8 pieces
flour, for dusting
2–3 tbsp. olive oil
1 large onion, (preferably Spanish),
   thickly sliced
2 bell peppers, deseeded and cut
   lengthwise into thick strips
2 garlic cloves

5 oz. spicy chorizo sausage, peeled,
   if necessary, and cut into
   1/2-inch pieces
1 tbsp. tomato paste
1 cup long-grain white rice or
   medium-grain Spanish rice,
   such as valencia
2 cups chicken stock

1 tsp. crushed dried chilies
1/2 tsp. dried thyme
4 oz. Bayonne or other air-dried ham,
   diced
12 dry-cured black olives
2 tbsp. chopped fresh flat-leaf parsley
salt and pepper

1 Dry the chicken pieces with paper towels. Put about 2 tablespoons flour in a plastic bag, season with salt and pepper, and add the chicken pieces. Seal the bag and shake to coat the chicken.

2 Heat 2 tablespoons of the oil in a large flameproof casserole over medium-high heat. Add the chicken and cook for about 15 minutes until well browned. Transfer to a plate.

3 Heat the remaining oil in the pan and add the onion and bell peppers. Reduce the heat to medium and stir-fry until beginning to color and soften. Add the garlic, chorizo, and tomato paste and continue stirring for about 3 minutes. Add the rice and cook for about 2 minutes, stirring to coat, until the rice is translucent.

4 Add the stock, crushed chilies, thyme, and salt and

pepper and stir. Bring to a boil. Return the chicken to the pan, pressing gently into the rice. Cover and cook over very low heat for about 45 minutes until the chicken and rice are tender.

5 Gently stir the ham, black olives, and half the parsley into the rice mixture. Re-cover and heat through for a further 5 minutes. Sprinkle with the remaining parsley and serve.

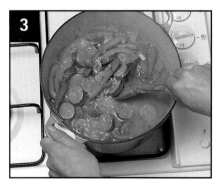

Pad Thai

All over Thailand and South East Asia, street stalls (even floating ones!) sell these simple delicious rice noodles, stir-fried to order. Serve with a selection of traditional accompaniments.

Serves 4

INGREDIENTS

8 oz. flat rice noodles (*sen lek*)
2 tbsp. peanut or vegetable oil
8 oz. boneless chicken breasts, skinned and thinly sliced
4 shallots, finely chopped
2 garlic cloves, finely chopped
4 scallions, cut on the diagonal into 2-inch pieces
12 oz. fresh white crab meat

1 cup fresh bean sprouts, rinsed
1 tbsp. preserved radish or fresh radish, finely diced
2–4 tbsp. roasted peanuts, chopped
fresh cilantro sprigs, to garnish

SAUCE:
3 tbsp. Thai fish sauce
2–3 tbsp. rice vinegar or cider vinegar
1 tbsp. chili bean sauce or oyster sauce
1 tbsp. toasted sesame oil
1 tbsp. palm sugar or light brown sugar
1/2 tsp. cayenne pepper or fresh red chili, thinly sliced

1 To make the sauce, whisk together the sauce ingredients in a small bowl and set aside.

2 Put the rice noodles in a large bowl and pour enough hot water over to cover; let stand for 15 minutes until softened. Drain, rinse, and drain again.

3 Heat the oil in a heavy-based wok over high heat until very

hot, but not smoking. Add the chicken strips and stir-fry for 1–2 minutes until they just begin to color. Using a slotted spoon, transfer to a plate. Reduce the heat to medium high.

4 Stir the shallots, garlic, and scallions into the wok and stir-fry for about 1 minute. Stir in the drained noodles, then the prepared sauce.

5 Return the reserved chicken to the pan with the crab meat, bean sprouts, and radish; toss well. Cook for about 5 minutes until heated through, tossing frequently. If the noodles begin to stick, add a little water.

6 Turn into a serving dish and sprinkle with the chopped peanuts. Garnish with cilantro and serve immediately.

Stir-fried Ginger Rice with Duck

For the best result, buy a 5 lb. duck, remove the breasts, and use the carcass to make a flavorful stock, simmering it with 2 quartered onions, some peppercorns, and sliced ginger root.

Serves 4–6

INGREDIENTS

2 duck breasts, cut into thin slices on the diagonal

2–3 tbsp. Japanese soy sauce

1 tbsp. mirin (sweet rice wine) or sherry

2 tsp. brown sugar

2-inch piece fresh ginger root, finely chopped or grated

4 tbsp. peanut oil

2 garlic cloves, crushed

1½ cups long-grain white or brown rice

3¼ cups chicken stock

4 oz. cooked lean ham, thinly sliced

6 oz. snow peas, cut diagonally in half

½ cup fresh bean sprouts, rinsed

8 scallions, thinly sliced on the diagonal

2–3 tbsp. chopped fresh cilantro

sweet or hot chili sauce (optional)

1 Put the duck in a shallow bowl with a tablespoon of soy sauce, the mirin, half the brown sugar, and one-third of the ginger. Stir to coat; marinate at room temperature.

2 Heat 2–3 tablespoons peanut oil in a large heavy-based saucepan over medium-high heat. Add the garlic and half the remaining ginger and stir-fry for about 1 minute until fragrant. Add the rice and cook for about 3 minutes, stirring, until translucent and beginning to color.

3 Add a scant 3 cups stock and a teaspoon of soy sauce and bring to a boil. Reduce the heat to very low and simmer, covered, for 20 minutes until the rice is tender and the liquid is absorbed. Do not uncover the pan, but remove from the heat and let stand.

4 Heat the remaining peanut oil in a large wok. Drain the duck breast and gently stir-fry for about 3 minutes until just colored. Add 1 tablespoon soy sauce and the rest of the sugar and cook for 1 minute; remove to a plate and keep warm.

5 Stir in the ham, snow peas, bean sprouts, scallions, the remaining ginger, and half the cilantro; add about ½ cup of the stock and stir-fry for 1 minute, or until the stock is almost reduced. Fork in the rice and toss together. Add a few drops of chili sauce, to taste.

6 To serve, pour into a serving dish, arrange the duck on top, and sprinkle with the remaining cilantro.

Azerbaijani Lamb Pilaf

This type of dish is popular from the Balkans, through Russia and the Middle East to India.
The saffron and pomegranate juice give it an exotic air.

Serves 4–6

INGREDIENTS

2–3 tbsp. oil

1 lb. 8 oz. boneless lamb shoulder, cut into 1-inch cubes

2 onions, coarsely chopped

1 tsp. ground cumin

1 cup arborio, long-grain, or basmati rice

1 tbsp. tomato paste

1 tsp. saffron threads

scant ½ cup pomegranate juice (see Cook's Tip)

3¾ cups lamb or chicken stock, or water

4 oz. dried apricots or prunes, ready soaked and halved

2 tbsp. raisins

salt and pepper

TO SERVE:

2 tbsp. chopped fresh mint

2 tbsp. chopped fresh watercress

1 Heat the oil in a large flameproof casserole or wide saucepan over high heat. Add the lamb in batches and cook for about 7 minutes, turning, until lightly browned.

2 Add the onions to the casserole, reduce the heat to medium high, and cook for about 2 minutes until beginning to soften. Add the cumin and rice and cook for about 2 minutes, stirring to coat well, until the rice is translucent. Stir in the tomato paste and the saffron threads.

3 Add the pomegranate juice and stock and bring to a boil, stirring once or twice. Add the apricots or prunes and raisins to the casserole, then stir together. Reduce the heat to low, cover, and simmer for 20–25 minutes until the lamb and rice are tender and the liquid is absorbed.

4 To serve, sprinkle the chopped mint and watercress over the pilaf and serve from the pan.

COOK'S TIP

Pomegranate juice is available from Middle Eastern grocery stores. If you cannot find it, substitute unsweetened grape or apple juice.

Louisiana "Dirty" Rice

This is a classic of American Southern cooking. The dish gets its name from the grayish color of the chicken livers and gizzards; nevertheless, it is delicious.

Serves 6

INGREDIENTS

6 oz. belly pork, diced or thickly sliced
  bacon
8 oz. chicken livers, trimmed, rinsed,
  dried, and chopped
8 oz. chicken gizzards, trimmed,
  rinsed, dried, and finely chopped
1 onion, finely chopped

1 stalk celery, finely chopped
1 green bell pepper, cored, deseeded,
  and chopped
3–4 garlic cloves, finely chopped
1 tsp. ground cumin
1 tsp. hot red pepper sauce, or to
  taste

1 cup long-grain white rice
2$\frac{1}{2}$ cups chicken stock
2–3 scallions, sliced
2–3 tbsp. chopped fresh flat-leaf
  parsley
salt and pepper

1 Cook the pork in a large heavy-based saucepan for about 7 minutes until it is crisp and golden. Using a slotted spoon, remove the bacon to a plate. Add the chicken livers and gizzards and cook, stirring occasionally, for about 5 minutes until tender and lightly golden. Transfer to the plate of pork.

2 Add the onion, celery, and bell pepper to the pan and cook for about 6 minutes, stirring frequently, until the vegetables are tender. Stir in the garlic, cumin, and hot pepper sauce and cook for a further 30 seconds.

3 Add the rice and cook, stirring, until translucent and well coated with the fat. Add the stock and season with salt and pepper.

4 Return the cooked bacon, chicken livers, and gizzards to the pan, stirring to blend. Cover and simmer gently for 20 minutes until the rice is tender and the liquid absorbed.

5 Fork half the scallions and the parsley into the rice and toss gently together. Transfer to a serving dish, sprinkle with the remaining scallions, and serve immediately.

COOK'S TIP

If you cannot find chicken gizzards, use all chicken livers. Gizzards are available in larger supermarkets or Spanish or Caribbean groceries.

Moros y Christianos

*Translated as "Black Beans and Rice," this classic Cuban recipe is a perfect
party dish—hearty, tasty, and easy to make ahead.*

Serves 8–10

INGREDIENTS

1 lb. dried small black beans, soaked
overnight in cold water
1 tbsp. vegetable or olive oil
8 oz. belly pork, diced or thickly sliced
bacon
1 large onion, preferably Spanish,
chopped
2 garlic cloves, finely chopped
2 ripe tomatoes, deseeded and chopped

1 tsp. ground cumin
$\frac{1}{2}$ tsp. dried crushed chilies, or to taste
2 fresh bay leaves or 1 dried bay leaf
1–2 tbsp. dark brown sugar
8 cups chicken stock
6 oz. spicy chorizo sausage, peeled if
necessary, cut into $\frac{1}{2}$-inch slices
2 lb. ham hock

1 cup long or medium-grain white
rice
1–2 tbsp. lime juice
1–2 tbsp. chopped fresh cilantro
(optional)
salt and pepper
lime wedges, to garnish

1 Drain the soaked beans and
rinse under cold water. Heat
the oil in a large flameproof
casserole over medium heat. Add
the belly pork or bacon and cook
for about 4 minutes until the fat is
rendered and the pork is
beginning to color.

2 Add the onion, garlic, and
tomatoes and cook, stirring
frequently, for about 10 minutes
until the vegetables are soft. Stir in
the cumin, crushed chilies, bay
leaves, and sugar.

3 Add the drained black beans
and stock. Add the chorizo,
then the ham hock, pushing it
down firmly. Bring to a boil,
skimming off any foam. Partially
cover, reduce the heat, and simmer
gently for about 2 hours, stirring
occasionally, until the meat and

beans are tender. Remove the ham
hock and cool slightly.

4 Meanwhile, bring a saucepan
of water to a boil. Add a pinch
of salt and sprinkle in the rice;
return to a boil. Reduce the heat
and simmer gently for about 20
minutes until the rice is tender.
Drain, rinse, and set aside.

5 Remove the meat from the
ham hock bone, cutting it
into pieces, and return it to the
beans. Stir in the cooked rice, lime
juice and half the cilantro. Adjust
the seasoning.

6 Transfer to a serving bowl and
sprinkle with the remaining
cilantro. Garnish with the lime
wedges and serve hot.

Baked Tomato Rice with Sausages

A great quick supper for the family,
this dish is incredibly simple to put together, yet is truly scrumptious!

Serves 4

INGREDIENTS

2 tbsp. vegetable oil
1 onion, coarsely chopped
1 red bell pepper, cored, deseeded, and
  chopped
2 garlic cloves, finely chopped
1/2 tsp. dried thyme

1 1/2 cups long-grain white rice
4 cups light chicken or vegetable
  stock
8 oz. can chopped tomatoes
1 bay leaf
2 tbsp. shredded fresh basil

6 oz. mature (sharp) Cheddar cheese,
  grated
2 tbsp. chopped fresh chives
4 pork sausages, cooked and cut into
  1/2-inch pieces
2–3 tbsp. freshly grated Parmesan
  cheese

1 Heat the oil in a large flame-proof casserole over medium heat. Add the onion and red bell pepper and cook for about 5 minutes, stirring frequently, until soft and lightly colored. Stir in the garlic and thyme and cook for a further minute.

2 Add the rice and cook, stirring frequently, for about 2 minutes until the rice is well coated and translucent. Stir in the stock, tomatoes, and bay leaf. Boil for 5 minutes until the stock is almost absorbed.

3 Stir in the basil, Cheddar cheese, chives, and pork sausages and bake, covered, in a preheated oven at 350°F for about 25 minutes.

4 Sprinkle with the Parmesan cheese and return to the oven, uncovered, for 5 minutes until the top is golden. Serve hot from the casserole.

VARIATION

For a vegetarian version, replace the pork sausages with a 14 oz. can of drained butter beans, kidney beans, or corn. Or try a mixture of sauteed mushrooms and zucchini.

Seafood Rice

This satisfying rice casserole, bursting with Mediterranean flavors, can be made with any combination of seafood you choose.

Serves 4–6

INGREDIENTS

4 tbsp. olive oil

16 large raw peeled shrimp, tails on if possible

8 oz. cleaned squid or cuttlefish, cut into $\frac{1}{2}$-inch slices

2 green bell peppers, deseeded and cut lengthwise into $\frac{1}{2}$-inch strips

1 large onion, finely chopped

4 garlic cloves, finely chopped

2 fresh bay leaves or 1 dried bay leaf

1 tsp. saffron threads

$\frac{1}{2}$ tsp. dried crushed chilies

2 cups arborio or valencia rice

1 cup dry white wine

$3\frac{3}{4}$ cups fish, light chicken or vegetable stock

12–16 littleneck clams, well scrubbed

12–16 large mussels, well scrubbed

salt and pepper

2 tbsp. chopped fresh flat-leaf parsley, to garnish

RED PEPPER SAUCE:

2–3 tbsp. olive oil

2 onions, finely chopped

4–6 garlic cloves, finely chopped

4–6 Italian roasted red bell peppers in olive oil (not in vinegar) or roasted, peeled, and coarsely chopped

$14\frac{1}{2}$ oz. can chopped tomatoes in juice

1–1$\frac{1}{2}$ tsp. hot paprika

salt

1 To make the red pepper sauce, heat the oil in a saucepan. Add the onions and cook for 6–8 minutes until golden. Stir in the garlic and cook for a minute. Add the remaining ingredients and simmer gently, stirring occasionally, for about 10 minutes. Process to form a smooth sauce; set aside and keep warm.

2 Heat half the oil in a wide pan over high heat. Add the shrimp and stir-fry for 2 minutes until pink. Transfer to a plate. Add the squid and stir-fry for about 2 minutes until just firm. Add to the shrimp.

3 Heat the remaining oil in the pan, add the green bell peppers and onion, and stir-fry for about 6 minutes until just tender. Stir in the garlic, bay leaves, saffron, and chilies and cook for 30 seconds. Add the rice and cook, stirring, until well coated.

4 Add the wine and stir until absorbed. Add the stock, salt, and pepper. Bring to a boil and cover. Simmer gently for about 20 minutes until the rice is just tender and the liquid is almost absorbed.

5 Add the clams and mussels. Re-cover and cook for about 10 minutes until the shells open. Stir in the shrimp and squid. Re-cover and heat through. Sprinkle with parsley; serve with the sauce.

Vietnamese Rice Paper Wraps

*A great idea for a party—just lay out the fillings,
with the two dipping sauces, and let guests assemble their own "wraps."*

Makes 20–30 wraps

INGREDIENTS

8 oz. cooked peeled shrimp

8 oz. salmon fillet, seared for
1 minute each side and cut into
1/4-inch slices

8 oz. tuna steak, seared for
1 minute each side and cut into
1/4-inch slices

2 ripe avocados, peeled, sliced and
sprinkled with lime juice

6–8 asparagus tips, blanched

1 small red onion, thinly sliced

16 scallions, sliced

12 black Niçoise olives, sliced

14 cherry tomatoes, halved

large bunch of cilantro, leaves
stripped from the stems

20–30 rice paper wrappers, preferably
7 inch circles

lime wedges

SPICED VINEGAR DIPPING SAUCE:

1/3 cup rice vinegar

2 tbsp. Thai fish sauce

2 tbsp. superfine sugar

1 garlic clove, finely chopped

2 red chilies, deseeded and thinly sliced

2 tbsp. chopped fresh cilantro

SOY DIPPING SAUCE:

1/2 cup Thai fish sauce

4–6 tbsp. lime juice

2 tbsp. Japanese soy sauce

2–3 tbsp. light brown sugar

1-inch piece fresh ginger root, finely
chopped

2–4 garlic cloves, minced

1 To make the dipping sauces, put the ingredients for each into separate bowls and stir together to blend.

2 Arrange the shrimp, fish, vegetables, and cilantro leaves on a large serving platter in groups, ready to use as different fillings for the wrappers. Cover loosely with plastic wrap and chill until ready to serve.

3 Dip each wrapper very briefly into a bowl of warm water to soften. Lay on clean dish towels to absorb any excess water, then pile onto a serving plate and cover with a damp dish towel.

4 To serve, allow each guest to fill their own wrappers. Offer lime wedges for squeezing over the fillings, and pass the dipping sauces separately.

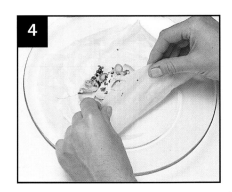

Fried Rice Parcels

This is a good way of using leftover rice to make an elegant appetizer or an unusual light lunch.
Vary the flavors and vegetables, or add other leftovers, finely chopped.

Serves 4

INGREDIENTS

8 large sheets of rice paper, cut into
   9-inch circles
1 egg white, lightly whisked
sesame seeds, for sprinkling
Soy Dipping Sauce (see page 72),
   to serve

FRIED RICE:
vegetable oil
1 tsp. cumin seeds
about 2 cups cooked white long-grain
   or basmati rice
1 tbsp. rice vinegar
1 tbsp. soy sauce
1 tsp. chili sauce, or to taste

2 scallions, finely chopped
4 oz. frozen peas, defrosted
2 tbsp. chopped fresh cilantro
3 oz. cooked ham or shrimp, diced
salt and pepper

1 Heat 1–2 tablespoons of the oil in a large heavy-based skillet. Add the cumin seeds and cook, stirring frequently, for about 1 minute until they begin to pop. Add the rice and stir-fry for 2–3 minutes.

2 Add the vinegar, soy sauce, and chili sauce, and toss with the rice. Add the scallions, peas, cilantro, and ham and stir-fry for 2 minutes to heat through.

Season with salt and pepper. Remove from the heat and cool slightly.

3 Fill a shallow pan with warm water and quickly draw each sheet of the rice paper through the water to wet lightly. Drain on dish towels.

4 Arrange the rice paper circles on a work surface and divide the mixture evenly among them.

Gather up the edges of the paper and twist to form parcels; tie each loosely with string. Transfer to a lightly oiled cookie sheet.

5 Brush the top and sides lightly with the egg white and sprinkle generously with sesame seeds. Bake in a preheated oven at 400°F for 15–20 minutes until the rice paper is golden. Serve the parcels hot, with the dipping sauce.

Mexican Tomato Rice with Peas

The tomatoes in this recipe give the rice its distinctive pinkish color.
The texture of the rice will be slightly "wet."

Serves 6–8

INGREDIENTS

2 cups long-grain white rice
1 large onion, chopped
2–3 garlic cloves, peeled and smashed
1½ cups canned Italian plum
   tomatoes
3–4 tbsp. olive oil
4 cups chicken stock

1 tbsp. tomato paste
1 Habanero or hot chili
6 oz. frozen green peas, defrosted
4 tbsp. chopped fresh cilantro
salt and pepper

TO SERVE:
1 large avocado, peeled, sliced, and
   sprinkled with lime juice
lime wedges
4 scallions, chopped
1 tbsp. chopped fresh cilantro

1 Cover the rice with hot water and let stand for 15 minutes. Drain, then rinse under cold running water.

2 Place the onion and garlic in a food processor and process until a smooth puree forms. Scrape into a small bowl and set aside. Put the tomatoes in the food processor and process until smooth, then strain into another bowl, pushing any solids through with a wooden spoon.

3 Heat the oil in a flameproof casserole over medium heat. Add the rice and cook for 4 minutes, stirring frequently, until golden and translucent. Add the onion puree and cook, stirring frequently, for a further 2 minutes. Add the stock and tomato paste and bring to a boil.

4 Using a pin or long needle, carefully pierce the chili in 2–3 places. Add to the rice, season with salt and pepper, and reduce the heat to low. Simmer, covered, for about 25 minutes until the rice is tender and the liquid just absorbed. Discard the chili, stir in the peas and cilantro, and cook for 5 minutes to heat through.

5 To serve, gently fork into a large shallow serving bowl. Arrange the avocado slices and lime wedges on top. Sprinkle the chopped scallions and cilantro over and serve at once.

Fidellos Tostados

The Sephardic Jews from Spain have been eating a very thin vermicelli-like pasta called fidellos for centuries. Cooked with rice, it is also popular in Greece.

Serves 6

INGREDIENTS

12 oz. vermicelli or angel hair pasta in
 coils, roughly broken
1/2 cup long-grain white rice
3 tbsp. extra-virgin olive oil
3/4 cup canned chopped tomatoes,
 drained

2 1/2 cups chicken stock or water, plus
 extra if necessary
1 bay leaf
1–2 tsp. chopped fresh oregano or
 1 tsp. dried oregano
1/2 tsp. dried thyme leaves

salt and pepper
1–2 tbsp. sprigs and chopped fresh
 oregano or thyme, to garnish

1 Put the pasta and rice in a dry, large, heavy-based saucepan or flameproof casserole over medium-high heat and cook for 5–7 minutes, stirring frequently, until light golden. (The pasta will break unevenly, but this does not matter.)

2 Stir in 2 tablespoons of the olive oil, together with the chopped tomatoes, stock, bay leaf, oregano, and thyme, then season with about a teaspoon of salt and pepper to taste.

3 Bring to a boil, reduce the heat to medium, and simmer for about 8 minutes, stirring frequently, to help unwind and separate the pasta coils.

4 Reduce the heat to low and cook, covered, for about 10 minutes until the rice and pasta are tender and all the liquid absorbed. If the rice and pasta are too firm, add about 1/2 cup more stock or water and continue to cook, covered, for a further 5 minutes. Remove from the heat.

5 Using a fork, fluff the rice and pasta into a warmed deep serving bowl and drizzle with the remaining oil. Sprinkle with the herbs and serve immediately.

Red Rice Pilaf with Roasted Root Vegetables

Red rice from the Camargue region in the South of France has an aromatic, nutty flavor which complements the robust flavors of the roasted vegetables.

Serves 4–6

INGREDIENTS

$^1/_2$ cup olive oil

grated rind and juice of 1 orange

2 tbsp. balsamic vinegar

2 tsp. coriander seeds, lightly crushed

1 bay leaf

$^1/_2$ tsp. crushed dried chilies, or to taste

8–10 small raw beets, trimmed, scrubbed and halved

9 oz. shallots or baby onions

6–8 baby parsnips, trimmed

4–6 baby carrots, trimmed

1 tsp. chopped fresh rosemary leaves

2 cups red Camargue rice

$3^3/_4$ cups hot chicken stock

1 red onion

1 small carrot, cut into matchstick strips

1 leek, cut into $^1/_2$-inch rounds

$^1/_2$ cup pine nuts, lightly roasted

1 tsp. light brown sugar

about 1 cup dried cranberries, sour cherries, or raisins, soaked in boiling water for 15 minutes

1–2 tbsp. chopped fresh cilantro

salt and pepper

TO SERVE:

1 cup sour cream

2 tbsp. chopped roasted walnuts

1 Put about 4 tablespoons of the olive oil in a large bowl and whisk in the orange rind and juice, vinegar, coriander seeds, bay leaf, and crushed chilies. Add the beets, shallots, parsnips, and carrots and stir to coat well.

2 Turn into a roasting pan and roast in a preheated oven at 400°F for 45–55 minutes until the vegetables are tender, turning occasionally. Remove from the oven, sprinkle with the rosemary and salt and pepper; keep warm.

3 Put the rice in a large saucepan with the hot stock. Place over medium-high heat and bring to a boil; reduce the heat to low and simmer, covered, for about 40 minutes until the rice is tender and the stock absorbed. Remove from the heat but do not uncover.

4 Heat the remaining oil in a large pan. Add the onion and carrot strips and cook for 8–10 minutes until tender. Add the leek, pine nuts, brown sugar, and cilantro and cook for 2–3 minutes until the vegetables are lightly caramelized. Drain the cranberries and stir into the vegetable mixture with the rice. Season with salt and pepper.

5 Arrange the roasted vegetables and rice on a serving platter and top with the sour cream. Sprinkle with the chopped walnuts and serve.

Curried Rice Patties with Tahini Dressing

Substantial and flavorful, these patties are a delicious alternative to beef burgers.
Leave the rice with a little bite to give extra texture.

Serves 4–6

INGREDIENTS

¹/₂ tsp. salt
¹/₃ cup basmati white or brown rice
2 tbsp. olive oil
1 red onion, finely chopped
2 garlic cloves
2 tsp. curry powder
¹/₂ tsp. crushed dried chili flakes
1 small red bell pepper, cored,
   deseeded and diced
4 oz. frozen peas, defrosted
1 small leek, finely chopped

1 ripe tomato, skinned, deseeded, and
   chopped
11 oz. can chickpeas, drained and
   rinsed
1¹/₂ cups fresh white breadcrumbs
1–2 tbsp. chopped fresh cilantro or
   mint
1 egg, lightly beaten
vegetable oil, for frying
salt and pepper
cucumber slices, to garnish
lime wedges, to serve

DRESSING:
¹/₂ cup tahini
2 garlic cloves, gently crushed
¹/₂ tsp. ground cumin, or to taste
pinch of cayenne pepper
5 tbsp. lemon juice
drizzle of extra-virgin olive oil
about ¹/₂ cup water

1 To make the dressing, blend the tahini, garlic, cumin, cayenne, and lemon juice in a food processor until creamy. Slowly pour in the oil, then gradually add water to make a creamy dressing.

2 Bring a saucepan of water to a boil. Add the salt and sprinkle in the rice; simmer for 15–20 minutes until the rice is just tender. Drain, rinse, and set aside.

3 Heat the olive oil in a large pan. Add the onion and garlic and cook until beginning to soften. Stir in the curry powder and chili and cook for 2 minutes. Add the bell pepper, peas, leek, and tomato and cook gently for 7 minutes until tender. Set aside.

4 Process the chickpeas in the food processor until smooth. Add half the vegetables and process again. Transfer to a large bowl and add the remaining vegetable mixture, breadcrumbs, cilantro, and egg; mix well. Stir in the rice and season well. Chill for 1 hour, then shape into 4–6 patties.

5 Fry the patties in oil for 6–8 minutes until golden. Garnish with cucumber slices and serve with the dressing and lime wedges.

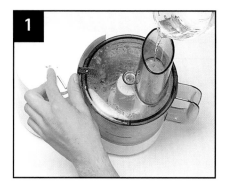

Spicy Potato-rice Pilaf

This spicy blend of potatoes, rice, and peas is rich enough to serve on its own or it can be served as part of an Indian meal. If you like it very spicy, serve with a cooling cucumber raita or yogurt.

Serves 4–6

INGREDIENTS

1 cup basmati rice, soaked in cold
  water for 20 minutes
2 tbsp. vegetable oil
$^1\!/_2$–$^3\!/_4$ tsp. cumin seeds
8 oz. potatoes, cut into $^1\!/_2$-inch pieces
8 oz. frozen peas, defrosted

1 green chili, deseeded and thinly
  sliced (optional)
$^1\!/_2$ tsp. salt
1 tsp. garam masala
$^1\!/_2$ tsp. ground turmeric
$^1\!/_4$ tsp. cayenne pepper

$2^1\!/_2$ cups water
2 tbsp. chopped fresh cilantro
1 red onion, finely chopped
natural yogurt, to serve

1 Rinse the soaked rice under cold running water until the water runs clear; drain and set aside.

2 Heat the oil in a large heavy-based saucepan over medium-high heat. Add the cumin seeds and stir for about 10 seconds until the seeds jump and color.

3 Add the potatoes, peas, and chili, if using, and stir-fry for about 3 minutes until the potatoes are just beginning to soften.

4 Add the rice and cook, stirring frequently, until well coated and beginning to turn translucent. Stir in the salt, garam masala, turmeric, and cayenne pepper, then add the water. Bring to a boil, stirring once or twice, then reduce the heat to medium and simmer, covered, until most of the water is absorbed and the surface is filled with little steam holes. Do not stir.

5 Reduce the heat to very low and, if possible, raise the pan about 1 inch above the heat source by resting on a ring. Cover and steam for about 10 minutes longer. Remove from the heat, uncover, and put a clean dish towel or paper towels over the rice; re-cover. Let stand for 5 minutes.

6 Gently fork the rice and potato mixture into a warmed serving bowl and sprinkle with the cilantro and chopped red onion. Serve hot, with yogurt passed separately.

Turkish Carrot Pilaf

Because of their bright golden color, carrots symbolize hope and prosperity in many cultures. They sweeten the rice in this delicious Turkish pilaf and add a slightly crunchy texture.

Serves 6

INGREDIENTS

4 tbsp. butter
2 carrots, coarsely grated
$\frac{1}{2}$ tsp. whole black peppercorns
pinch of salt

4–6 ready-soaked dried apricots,
  thinly sliced (optional)
1 tsp. sugar
2 cups long-grain white rice
3 cups chicken stock

1–2 tbsp. chopped green pistachios,
  for sprinkling (optional)

1 Melt the butter in a large, heavy-based saucepan over medium heat. Add the grated carrots and whole peppercorns with a pinch of salt and cook, stirring frequently, for about 3 minutes until the carrots begin to soften.

2 Add the apricots, if using, and sprinkle with the sugar, stirring to combine. Stir in the rice and cook, stirring frequently, for about 3 minutes until the rice is coated with butter and is translucent.

3 Pour in the stock and bring to a boil. Reduce the heat to low and simmer, covered, for 20–25 minutes until the rice is tender and the stock is completely absorbed. Remove from the heat and uncover. Place a folded dish towel or paper towels over the rice and re-cover. Let stand for about 10 minutes for any steam to be absorbed.

4 Fork the rice into a shallow serving bowl and shape into a rounded dome; sprinkle with the pistachios, if using, and serve hot.

COOK'S TIP

As an alternative serving idea, spoon the pilaf into an oiled ring mold, pressing lightly to compress the rice. Cover the mold with an upturned serving plate and, holding the plate and mold firmly together, invert quickly, giving a good shake. Gently remove the mold. Fill the center with chopped pistachios and garnish with a sprig of parsley and cooked carrot strips.

Coconut-scented Brown Rice

In this basic recipe, brown rice is cooked slowly by the absorption method, producing a tender, creamy rice with lots of flavor. An excellent accompaniment to broiled chicken, pork, or even fish.

Serves 4–6

INGREDIENTS

1½ cups water
1 cup coconut milk
1 tsp. salt

1 cup long-grain brown rice
1 lemon
1 cinnamon stick

about 15 whole cloves
1 tbsp. chopped fresh parsley
fresh coconut shavings (optional)

1 Bring the water to a boil in a heavy-based saucepan and whisk in the coconut milk. Return the liquid to a boil, add the salt, and sprinkle in the rice.

2 Pare 2–3 strips of lemon rind and add to the saucepan with the cinnamon stick and the cloves.

3 Reduce the heat to low, cover, and simmer gently for about 45 minutes until the rice is tender and the liquid is completely absorbed. Uncover and leave the rice over high heat for about 1 minute, to allow any steam to escape and the rice to dry out a little bit.

4 Remove the cloves, if desired, then sprinkle with the herbs and coconut, if using; fork into a warmed serving bowl and serve.

VARIATION

The whole cloves can be replaced with a pinch of ground allspice.

COOK'S TIP

This technique can be used to cook white rice as well, but the fuller flavor of brown rice works well with the warm flavor of the spices.

VARIATION

For a more South-East Asian flavor, use 1 red chili, pierced in 2–3 places with a pin, a bruised lime leaf, and a 3-inch piece of lemon grass, lightly crushed, instead of the lemon and cloves.

Fragrant Orange Basmati Rice

This delicious rice, scented with star anise for a slightly exotic effect, is excellent served with Mediterranean and Middle Eastern meat stews.

Serves 4–6

INGREDIENTS

1–2 tbsp. butter
3–4 shallots, finely chopped
1 cup basmati rice
1-inch piece of fresh ginger root, peeled

1–2 fresh bay leaves, lightly bruised
2 star anise
1 small cinnamon stick
grated rind and juice of 1 orange
1 tbsp. raisins, finely chopped

1¼ cups light chicken stock or water
salt and pepper
fresh cilantro leaves, to garnish (optional)

1 Melt the butter in a heavy-based saucepan placed over medium heat. Add the shallots and cook for 2–3 minutes until beginning to soften.

2 Add the rice and cook, stirring frequently, for 3 minutes until the rice is well coated with the butter and is translucent. Using a large heavy knife, crush the piece of ginger lightly. Add to the pan with the bay leaves, star anise, and cinnamon stick. Add the grated rind and orange juice and the raisins and stir.

3 Add the stock and bring to a boil. Season with salt and pepper and reduce the heat. Cover and cook over low heat for 15–18 minutes until the rice is tender and the liquid completely absorbed. Remove from the heat, uncover and place a clean dish towel over the rice. Re-cover and stand for up to 20 minutes.

4 Fork the rice into a serving bowl and remove the bay leaves, star anise, and cinnamon stick (or keep them in for decoration). Sprinkle the top

with a few cilantro leaves, if desired, and serve hot.

COOK'S TIP

Most packaged brands of basmati do not need washing and soaking. However, it does not hurt to wash the rice; it simply removes any starch. Cover the rice with water and soak for about 20 minutes, stirring occasionally. Drain, then rinse under cold running water until the water runs clear. Drain and proceed with the recipe.

Lemon-scented Rice with Mint

The fresh clean flavors of this pilaf make it an ideal accompaniment for a wide variety of dishes, from plain roasted meats to exotic curries and stews.

Serves 6–8

INGREDIENTS

2 tbsp. olive oil or butter
2–4 scallions, finely chopped
3–4 tbsp. chopped fresh mint
1½ cups long-grain white rice

2¼ cups chicken stock, preferably
  homemade
1 lemon
salt and pepper

TO GARNISH:
2–3 mint sprigs
thin lemon and lime slices

1 Heat the oil or butter in a medium heavy-based saucepan over medium-high heat. Add the scallions and mint and cook, stirring, for about 1 minute until brightly colored and fragrant.

2 Add the rice and cook, stirring frequently, for about 2 minutes until well coated with the oil or butter and just translucent. Add the chicken stock and bring to a boil, stirring once or twice. Season with salt and pepper to taste.

3 Pare 3–4 strips of lemon rind and add to the pan; squeeze the juice from the lemon and stir into the rice and stock.

4 When the stock comes to a boil, reduce the heat to low and simmer gently, tightly covered, for about 20 minutes until the rice is tender and the stock absorbed. Remove the pan from the heat and let stand for 5–10 minutes.

5 Fork the rice into a serving bowl, garnish with mint and lemon and lime slices. Serve hot.

COOK'S TIP

This basic technique for pilaf rice can be used with other flavor combinations and herbs. The important thing is to fry the rice until well coated and add just enough water to be absorbed by the rice.

Fruity Rice Stuffing

This rich fruit-filled stuffing, inspired by a Turkish pilaf, is a wonderful way to use leftover rice.
Here it is used with Cornish hens, but it is also delicious with lamb, goose, duck and game birds.

Serves 4

INGREDIENTS

4 fresh Cornish game hens
4–6 tbsp. butter, melted

STUFFING:
1 cup port
11 cup raisins
1 cup dried no-soak apricots, sliced
2–3 tbsp. extra-virgin olive oil
1 onion, finely chopped

1 stalk celery, thinly sliced
2 garlic cloves, finely chopped
1 tsp. ground cinnamon
1 tsp. dried oregano
1 tsp. dried mint or basil
$\frac{1}{2}$ tsp. allspice or $\frac{1}{4}$ tsp. cloves
8 oz. unsweetened chestnuts, canned
    or vacuum-packed
1 cup long-grain white rice, cooked

grated rind and juice of 2 oranges
$1\frac{1}{2}$ cups chicken stock
$\frac{1}{2}$ cup walnut halves, lightly toasted
    and chopped
2 tbsp. chopped fresh mint
2 tbsp. chopped fresh flat-leaf parsley
salt and pepper

1 To make the stuffing, combine the port, raisins, and apricots in a small bowl and let stand for about 15 minutes.

2 Heat the oil in a large heavy-based saucepan. Add the onion and celery and cook for 3–4 minutes. Add the garlic, all the spices, and the chestnuts and cook for about 4 minutes, stirring occasionally. Add the rice and half the orange rind and juice, then pour in the stock. Simmer gently for 5 minutes until most of the liquid is absorbed.

3 Drain the raisins and apricots, reserving the port, and stir into the rice mixture with the walnuts, mint, and parsley; cook for a further 2 minutes. Season with salt and pepper, then remove from the heat and cool.

4 Rub the Cornish game hens inside and out with salt and pepper. Lightly fill the cavity of each bird with the stuffing; do not pack too tightly. Tie the legs of each bird together, tucking in the tail. Form extra stuffing into balls.

5 Arrange the birds in a roasting pan with any stuffing balls and brush with melted butter. Drizzle any remaining butter around the pan. Pour the remaining orange rind and juice and the reserved port over.

6 Roast in a preheated oven at 350°F for about 45 minutes, basting, until cooked. Transfer to a platter, cover with foil, and let rest for 5 minutes. Serve with any pan juices.

Mixed Rice Stuffing with Wild Mushrooms

*Prepared by the pilaf method to infuse both rices with as much flavor as possible,
this stuffing is also excellent as a side dish.*

Makes enough to stuff 1 large chicken or small turkey

INGREDIENTS

4 tbsp. butter or oil
6 shallots, finely chopped
1 cup wild rice
2½ cups chicken stock
1 bay leaf
½ tsp. dried thyme or 2-3 sprigs fresh

1 cup long-grain white rice
2 oz. dried wild mushrooms
8 oz. fresh mushrooms, sliced
2 garlic cloves, finely chopped
3-4 tbsp. Madeira wine

½ cup pecan or walnut halves, toasted
and coarsely chopped
3-4 tbsp. chopped fresh flat-leaf
parsley
2 tbsp. chopped fresh chives
salt and pepper

1 Heat half the butter or oil in a large saucepan. Add half the shallots and cook until beginning to soften. Stir in the wild rice to coat, then add 1½ cups of the chicken stock, the bay leaf, and thyme, and bring to a boil. Simmer gently, covered, for about 20 minutes until the stock is absorbed. The wild rice will not be completely cooked.

2 Add the white rice and the remaining stock and season with salt and pepper. Bring to a boil again, stirring once or twice, then simmer gently, covered, for 20–25 minutes until the stock is absorbed and all the rice is tender. Remove from the heat and let stand, covered, for 10–15 minutes.

3 Meanwhile, cover the wild mushrooms with boiling water and let soften for about 30 minutes. Lift the mushrooms out and pat dry. Slice thinly.

4 Heat the remaining butter or oil in a large skillet. Add the remaining shallots and cook for 3 minutes. Add the fresh mushrooms, garlic, and Madeira and stir-fry for 3–4 minutes until golden. Stir in the wild mushrooms and cook, stirring occasionally, until all the liquid is absorbed. Pour into a large bowl.

5 Using a fork, fluff the rice into the bowl with the mushrooms, add the chopped nuts, parsley, and chives and adjust the seasoning; toss together. Cool before using as a stuffing.

Risottos

One of the great gastronomic feats of Italian cooking, risotto is made with a special rice to create a deliciously creamy dish. It is surprisingly simple to make, but does require a little patience because it involves slow cooking and constant stirring. As long as you use the correct rice and a good homemade stock, and take your time, you'll be on your way to making a perfect risotto!

The recipes in this chapter illustrate the versatility of risotto. Here you'll find something for every occasion—Easy Cheesy Risotto with Parmesan shows you the basic, easy-to-make method; risotto with asparagus or wild mushrooms is guaranteed to give a mid-week meal a lift, while glamorous Champagne Risotto and interesting Black Risotto or Fennel Risotto with Vodka make memorable dinner party dishes. Risotto flavored with sun-dried tomatoes and Italian cheese, or Minted Risotto with Herbs, makes perfect food for family gatherings.

As a change from the classic risotto, try scrumptious Cheese-topped Risotto Tart with Spinach, or little Arrancini, irresistible fried risotto balls. There's even a tasty oven-baked risotto, with pancetta and mushrooms.

Easy Cheesy Risotto with Parmesan

Although this is the easiest, most basic risotto, it is one of the most delicious. Because there are few ingredients, use the best of each.

Serves 4–6

INGREDIENTS

4–5 tbsp. unsalted butter
1 onion, finely chopped
1½ cups arborio or carnaroli rice
½ cup dry white vermouth or white wine

5 cups chicken or vegetable stock, simmering
1 cup freshly grated Parmesan cheese, plus extra for sprinkling

salt and pepper

1 Heat about 2 tbsp. of the butter in a large heavy-based saucepan over medium heat. Add the onion and cook for about 2 minutes until just beginning to soften. Add the rice and cook for about 2 minutes, stirring frequently, until translucent and well coated with the butter.

2 Pour in the vermouth; it will bubble and steam rapidly and evaporate almost immediately. Add a ladleful (about 1 cup) of the simmering stock and cook, stirring constantly, until the stock is absorbed.

3 Continue adding the stock, about half a ladleful at a time, allowing each addition to be absorbed before adding the next—never allow the rice to cook "dry." This should take 20–25 minutes. The risotto should have a creamy consistency and the rice grains should be tender, but still firm to the bite.

4 Remove the pan from the heat and stir in the remaining butter and Parmesan. Season with salt and a little pepper, to taste. Cover, stand for about 1 minute, then serve immediately with extra Parmesan for sprinkling.

COOK'S TIP

If you prefer not to use butter, soften the onion in 2 tablespoons olive oil and stir in about 2 tablespoons extra-virgin olive oil with the Parmesan at the end.

Risotto with Asparagus

An Italian classic, this simple recipe makes a stylish lunch or supper dish.
It's worth using the best asparagus you can find.

Serves 6

INGREDIENTS

2 lb. fresh asparagus, washed

2 tbsp. sunflower or other vegetable oil

6 tbsp. unsalted butter

2 shallots or 1 small onion, finely chopped

2 cups arborio or carnaroli rice

6¼ cups light chicken or vegetable stock, simmering

1 cup freshly grated Parmesan cheese

salt and pepper

Parmesan shavings, to garnish (optional)

1 Lightly peel the stems of the asparagus; trim off the woody ends. Cut the tips off each stalk and set aside. Cut the remaining stems into 1-inch pieces.

2 Add the asparagus stem pieces to a pan of boiling water and boil for 2 minutes. Add the asparagus tips and boil for about 1 minute until tender-crisp; do not overcook. Rinse under cold running water and set aside.

3 Heat the oil with half the butter in a large heavy-based saucepan. Add the shallots and cook gently for about 2 minutes until softened. Add the rice and cook, stirring frequently, for about 2 minutes until the rice is translucent and well coated.

4 Add a ladleful (about 1 cup) of the simmering stock; it will bubble and steam rapidly. Cook, stirring constantly, until the stock is completely absorbed.

5 Continue adding the stock, about half a ladleful at a time, allowing each addition to be absorbed before adding the next—never allow the rice to cook "dry." This should take 20–25 minutes. The risotto should have a creamy consistency and the rice should be tender, but firm to the bite.

6 Heat the asparagus tips in the stock. Stir the stems into the risotto with the last ladleful of stock, the remaining butter, and Parmesan. Remove from the heat and stir in the asparagus tips and season if necessary. Serve with Parmesan shavings, if desired.

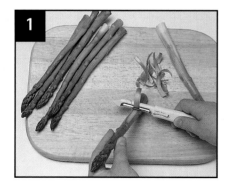

Lemon Risotto with Peas & Mint

Fresh peas and mint are added to this light and lemony risotto, which is excellent served as a first course for a summery meal.

Serves 4–6

INGREDIENTS

6¼ cups chicken stock
4–5 fresh mint sprigs
2 tbsp. extra-virgin olive oil
6 tbsp. unsalted butter
2–3 large shallots, finely chopped

1½ cups arborio or carnaroli rice
grated rind and juice of 1 large
  unwaxed lemon
6 oz fresh shelled peas,
  lightly cooked

⅔ cup freshly grated Parmesan cheese
salt and pepper
lemon wedges, to garnish

1 Bring the stock to a boil in a large saucepan. Strip the leaves from the mint sprigs and set aside; gently "bruise" the mint stems and add to the stock. Reduce the heat and keep the stock at a gentle simmer.

2 Heat the oil and half the butter in a large heavy-based saucepan over medium heat. Add the shallots and cook for about 2 minutes until soft. Add the rice and cook, stirring frequently, for about 2 minutes until the rice is translucent and well coated.

3 Leaving aside the mint stems, add a ladleful (about 1 cup) of the simmering stock; it will steam and bubble rapidly. Cook, stirring constantly, until the stock is absorbed.

4 Continue adding the stock, about half a ladleful at a time, allowing each addition to be absorbed before adding the next. This should take 20–25 minutes. The risotto should have a creamy consistency and the rice should be tender but firm to the bite.

5 Stir in the lemon rind and juice and the peas; cook until heated through, adding a little more stock or water if the risotto becomes too thick. Remove the pan from the heat and stir in the Parmesan and remaining butter. Season to taste with salt and pepper.

6 Chop the reserved mint leaves and stir into the risotto. Serve immediately with lemon wedges.

Minted Green Risotto with Herbs

This tasty risotto gets its vibrant green colour from the spinach and mint. Serve with Italian-style rustic bread and salad for an informal supper.

Serves 6

INGREDIENTS

2 tbsp. unsalted butter

1 lb. fresh shelled peas, or defrosted frozen peas

2 lb. 4 oz. fresh young spinach leaves, washed and drained

1 bunch fresh mint, leaves stripped from stalks

2 tbsp. chopped fresh basil

2 tbsp. chopped fresh oregano

large pinch of freshly grated nutmeg

4 tbsp. mascarpone or heavy cream

2 tbsp. vegetable oil

1 onion, finely chopped

4 stalks celery, including leaves, finely chopped

2 garlic cloves, finely chopped

1/2 tsp. dried thyme

1 1/2 cups arborio or carnaroli rice

1/4 cup dry white vermouth

4 cups light chicken or vegetable stock, simmering

1 cup freshly grated Parmesan cheese

1 Heat half the butter in a deep skillet over medium-high heat until sizzling. Add the peas, spinach, mint leaves, basil, and oregano; season with the nutmeg. Cook for about 3 minutes, stirring frequently, until the spinach and mint leaves are wilted. Cool slightly.

2 Pour the spinach mixture into a food processor and process for 15 seconds. Add the mascarpone and process again for about 1 minute. Transfer to a bowl and set aside.

3 Heat the oil and remaining butter in a large, heavy-based saucepan over medium heat. Add the onion, celery, garlic, and thyme and cook for about 2 minutes until the vegetables are softened. Add the rice and cook, stirring frequently, for about 2 minutes until the rice is translucent and well coated.

4 Add the vermouth to the rice; it will bubble and steam rapidly. When it is almost absorbed, add a ladleful (about 1 cup) of the simmering stock. Cook, stirring constantly, until the stock is completely absorbed.

5 Continue adding the stock, about half a ladleful at a time, allowing each addition to be absorbed before adding the next. This should take 20–25 minutes. The risotto should have a creamy consistency and the rice should be just tender. Stir in the spinach-cream mixture and the Parmesan. Serve immediately.

Fennel Risotto with Vodka

The alcohol in the vodka cooks out but leaves a pleasant, tantalizing flavor that complements the cool sweetness of the fennel.

Serves 4–6

INGREDIENTS

2 large fennel bulbs
2 tbsp. vegetable oil
6 tbsp. unsalted butter
1 large onion, finely chopped
1¾ cups arborio or carnaroli rice

⅔ cup vodka (or lemon-flavored vodka, if you can find it)
5⅔ cups light chicken or vegetable stock, simmering
⅔ cup freshly grated Parmesan cheese

5–6 tbsp. lemon juice
salt and pepper

1 Trim the fennel, reserving the fronds for the garnish, if wished. Cut the bulbs in half lengthwise and remove the V-shaped cores; coarsely chop the flesh. (If you like, add any of the fennel trimmings to the stock for extra flavor.)

2 Heat the oil and half the butter in a large heavy-based saucepan over medium heat. Add the onion and fennel and cook for about 2 minutes, stirring frequently, until the vegetables are softened. Add the rice and cook for about 2 minutes, stirring frequently, until the rice is translucent and well coated.

3 Pour in the vodka; it will bubble rapidly and evaporate almost immediately. Add a ladleful (about 1 cup) of the stock. Cook, stirring constantly, until the stock is absorbed.

4 Continue adding the stock, about half a ladleful at a time, allowing each addition to be absorbed before adding the next— never allow the rice to cook "dry."

This should take 20–25 minutes. The risotto should have a creamy consistency and the rice should be tender, but firm to the bite.

5 Stir in the remaining butter, with the Parmesan and lemon juice. Remove from the heat, cover, and stand for 1 minute. Serve immediately, garnished with a few of the fennel fronds, if desired.

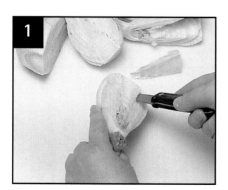

Risotto with Cannellini Beans

The Italians, particularly the Tuscans, love dishes made with beans.
This recipe combines beans and rice to make a rich, creamy risotto with a great flavor.

Serves 6–8

INGREDIENTS

10½ oz. cannellini or white kidney
  beans, soaked and cooked according
  to package instructions
2–3 tbsp. olive oil
1 large red (or sweet white) onion,
  finely chopped
3–4 stalks celery, finely chopped

4 oz. pancetta or thick-cut smoky
  bacon
2–3 garlic cloves, minced
¾ tsp. dried oregano or 1 tbsp.
  chopped fresh oregano
2 cups arborio or carnaroli rice
4 cups chicken stock, simmering

4 tbsp. unsalted butter at room
  temperature
1⅓ cups freshly grated Parmesan
  cheese
salt and pepper

1 Mash, or press through a food mill, half of the cannellini beans and set aside.

2 Heat the olive oil in a large heavy-based saucepan over medium heat. Add the onion and celery and cook for about 2 minutes until softened. Add the pancetta, garlic, and oregano and cook for a further 1–2 minutes, stirring occasionally. Add the rice and cook, stirring frequently, for about 2 minutes until it is translucent and well coated with the oil.

3 Add a ladleful (about 1 cup) of the simmering stock; it will bubble and steam rapidly. Cook, stirring constantly, until the stock is absorbed.

4 Continue adding the stock, about half a ladleful at a time, allowing each addition to be absorbed before adding the next. This should take 20–25 minutes.

The risotto should have a creamy consistency and the rice should be tender, but still firm to the bite.

5 Stir in the beans and the bean puree, season with salt and pepper and heat through. Add a little more stock if necessary.

6 Remove from the heat and stir in the butter and half the Parmesan. Cover and let stand for about 1 minute. Serve with the remaining Parmesan sprinkled over.

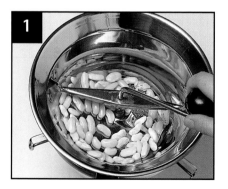

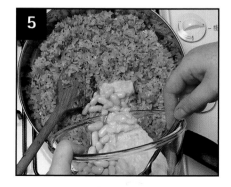

Champagne Risotto

This deluxe dish, with its pronounced Champagne flavor, is one to reserve for special occasions. Serve the rest of the wine with the dish, as the perfect accompaniment!

Serves 4–6

INGREDIENTS

2 tbsp. vegetable oil
8 tbsp. unsalted butter
2 shallots, finely chopped
1½ cups arborio or carnaroli rice

about 2½ cups Champagne or dry
 sparkling white wine
3 cups light chicken stock, simmering
⅔ cup freshly grated Parmesan cheese

salt and pepper
4–6 large cooked shrimp, to garnish
 (optional)

1 Heat the oil and half the butter in a large heavy-based saucepan over medium heat. Add the shallots and cook for about 2 minutes, until softened. Add the rice and cook, stirring frequently, for about 2 minutes until the rice is translucent and well coated (see Cook's Tip).

2 Pour in half the Champagne; it will bubble and steam rapidly. Cook, stirring constantly, until the liquid is absorbed. Add a ladleful (about 1 cup) of the simmering stock to the pan and cook, stirring constantly, until the liquid is absorbed.

3 Continue adding the stock, about half a ladleful at a time, allowing each addition to be absorbed before adding the next— never allow the rice to cook "dry." This should take 20–25 minutes. The risotto should have a creamy consistency and the rice should be tender, but firm to the bite.

4 Stir in the remaining champagne and cook for a further 2–3 minutes. Remove from the heat and stir in the remaining butter and Parmesan. Season with salt and pepper to taste.

5 Spoon the risotto into serving bowls and garnish each portion with a prawn (shrimp), if desired. Serve immediately.

COOK'S TIP

It is important to heat and coat the rice at this stage as it will help give the rice its creamy texture.

Wild Mushroom Risotto

Distinctive-tasting wild mushrooms, so popular in Italy,
give this dish a wonderful, robust flavor.

Serves 6

INGREDIENTS

2 oz. dried porcini or morel
  mushrooms
about 1 lb. 2 oz. mixed fresh wild
  mushrooms, such as porcini, girolles,
  horse mushrooms, and chanterelles,
  cleaned and halved if large

4 tbsp. olive oil
3–4 garlic cloves, finely chopped
4 tbsp. unsalted butter
1 onion, finely chopped
1¾ cups arborio or carnaroli rice
¼ cup dry white vermouth

5 cups chicken stock, simmering
1⅓ cups freshly grated Parmesan
  cheese
4 tbsp. chopped fresh flat-leaf parsley
salt and pepper

1   Cover the dried mushrooms with boiling water. Soak for 30 minutes, then carefully lift out and pat dry. Strain the soaking liquid through a strainer lined with a paper towel, and set aside.

2   Trim the wild mushrooms and gently brush clean.

3   Heat 3 tablespoons of the oil in a large skillet until hot. Add the fresh mushrooms, and stir-fry for 1–2 minutes. Add the garlic and the soaked mushrooms and cook for 2 minutes, stirring frequently. Scrape onto a plate and set aside.

4   Heat the remaining oil and half the butter in a large heavy-based saucepan. Add the onion and cook for about 2 minutes until softened. Add the rice and cook, stirring frequently, for about 2 minutes until translucent and well coated.

5   Add the vermouth to the rice. When almost absorbed, add a ladleful (about 1 cup) of the simmering stock. Cook, stirring constantly, until the liquid is absorbed.

6   Continue adding the stock, about half a ladleful at a time, allowing each addition to be absorbed before adding the next. This should take 20–25 minutes. The risotto should have a creamy consistency and the rice should be tender, but firm to the bite.

7   Add half the dried-mushroom soaking liquid to the risotto and stir in the mushrooms. Season with salt and pepper, and add more mushroom liquid if necessary. Remove from the heat; stir in the remaining butter, Parmesan, and parsley. Serve immediately.

Risotto Primavera

This is a nice way to use those first green vegetables which signal the spring, la primavera.
Feel free to add other favorite vegetables, if you like.

Serves 6–8

INGREDIENTS

8 oz. fresh thin asparagus spears, well rinsed

4 tbsp. olive oil

6 oz. young green beans, cut into 1-inch pieces

6 oz. young zucchini, quartered and cut into 1-inch lengths

8 oz. fresh shelled peas

1 onion, finely chopped

1–2 garlic cloves, finely chopped

1¾ cups arborio or carnaroli rice

6¼ cups chicken stock, simmering, plus extra 2 tbsp.

4 scallions, cut into 1-inch lengths

4 tbsp. unsalted butter

1⅓ cups freshly grated Parmesan cheese

2 tbsp. chopped fresh chives

2 tbsp. fresh shredded basil

salt and pepper

1 Trim the woody ends of the asparagus and cut off the tips. Cut the stems into 1-inch pieces and set aside with the tips.

2 Heat 2 tablespoons of the olive oil in a large skillet over high heat, until very hot. Add the asparagus, beans, zucchini, and peas and stir-fry for 3–4 minutes until they are bright green and just beginning to soften. Set aside.

3 Heat the remaining olive oil in a large heavy-based saucepan over medium heat. Add the onion and cook for about 1 minute until it begins to soften. Stir in the garlic and cook for 30 seconds. Add the rice and cook, stirring frequently, for 2 minutes until translucent and coated with oil.

4 Add a ladleful (about 1 cup) of the hot stock; the stock will bubble rapidly. Cook, stirring

constantly, until the stock is absorbed.

5 Continue adding the stock, about half a ladleful at a time, allowing each addition to be absorbed before adding the next—never allow the rice to cook "dry." This should take 20–25 minutes. The risotto should have a creamy consistency and the rice should be tender, but firm to the bite.

6 Stir in the stir-fried vegetables and scallions with a little more stock. Cook for 2 minutes, stirring frequently, then season with salt and pepper. Stir in the butter, Parmesan, chives and basil. Remove from the heat, cover, and let stand for about 1 minute. Garnish with scallions, if desired. Serve immediately.

Roasted Pumpkin Risotto

*The combination of sweet creamy pumpkin with
the slight saltiness of gorgonzola and the pungency of sage is delicious.*

Serves 6

INGREDIENTS

4 tbsp. olive oil

4 tbsp. unsalted butter, cut into small
   pieces

1 lb. pumpkin flesh, cut into $\frac{1}{2}$-inch
   cubes

$\frac{3}{4}$ tsp. rubbed sage

2 garlic cloves, finely chopped

2 tbsp. lemon juice

2 large shallots, finely chopped

$1\frac{3}{4}$ cups arborio or carnaroli rice

$\frac{1}{4}$ cup dry white vermouth

5 cups chicken stock, simmering

vegetable oil, for frying

$\frac{2}{3}$ cup freshly grated Parmesan cheese

$10\frac{1}{2}$ oz. gorgonzola dolce or Saga
   Blue cheese, cut into small pieces

salt and pepper

celery leaves, to garnish

---

1 Put half the olive oil and about 1 tbsp. of the butter in a roasting pan and heat in a preheated oven at 400°F.

2 Add the pumpkin to the pan and sprinkle with the sage, half the garlic, and salt and pepper. Toss together and roast for about 10 minutes until just softened and beginning to caramelize. Transfer to a plate.

3 Roughly mash about half the cooked pumpkin with the lemon juice and reserve with the remaining diced pumpkin.

4 Heat the remaining oil and 1 tbsp. of the butter in a large, heavy-based saucepan over medium heat. Stir in the shallots and remaining garlic and cook for about 1 minute. Add the rice and cook, stirring, for about 2 minutes until well coated.

5 Pour in the vermouth; it will bubble and steam rapidly. Add a ladleful (about 1 cup) of the simmering stock and cook, stirring constantly, until the stock is absorbed.

6 Continue adding the stock, about half a ladleful at a time, allowing each addition to be absorbed before adding the next—never allow the rice to cook "dry." This should take 20–25 minutes. The risotto should have a creamy consistency and the rice should be tender, but firm to the bite.

7 Stir all the pumpkin into the risotto with the remaining butter and the Parmesan. Remove from the heat and fold in the diced gorgonzola. Serve at once, garnished with celery leaves.

Truffle Risotto

If you feel like splashing out on a luxurious dish, this is the one for you! Traditionally this risotto is made with white truffles, but black truffles are used in this version as they are more widely available.

Serves 6

INGREDIENTS

2 leeks
8 tbsp. unsalted butter
1¹/₂ cups arborio or carnaroli rice
5 cups chicken stock, simmering
¹/₄ cup dry white vermouth or
   white wine

¹/₂ cup heavy cream
freshly grated nutmeg
1¹/₃ cups freshly grated Parmesan
   cheese
4–6 oz. fresh black truffles, brushed
   clean
¹/₄–¹/₃ cup truffle oil (optional)

salt and ¹/₄–¹/₂ tsp. ground white
   pepper

1 Slice the leeks in half lengthwise, then shred thinly.

2 Heat half the butter in a large heavy-based pan over medium heat. Add the leeks and cook for about 1 minute until just starting to soften. Add the rice and cook, stirring, until translucent and well coated in butter.

3 Add a ladleful (about 1 cup) of the hot stock; it will bubble and steam rapidly.

Cook, stirring, until the stock is absorbed.

4 Continue adding the stock, about half a ladleful at a time, allowing each addition to be absorbed before adding the next. This should take 20–25 minutes. The risotto should have a creamy consistency and the rice should be tender, but firm to the bite.

5 Just before the rice is cooked, stir in the vermouth and

cream. Season with a little nutmeg, salt, and white pepper. Continue cooking for 3–4 minutes until the liquid is absorbed. Remove from the heat and stir in the Parmesan and remaining butter.

6 Spoon into serving dishes and shave equal amounts of truffle over each portion. Drizzle a little truffle oil over, if using.

Beet, Dried Cherry, & Red Wine Risotto

*The beets and red wine give this risotto its stunning "hot pink" color
and also impart a rich sweet flavor that is unusual but surprisingly delicious.*

Serves 4–6

INGREDIENTS

1 cup dried sour cherries or dried
   cranberries
1 cup fruity red wine, such as
   Valpolicella
3 tbsp. olive oil
1 large red onion, finely chopped
2 stalks celery, finely chopped

$^1/_2$ tsp. dried thyme
1 garlic clove, finely chopped
$1^3/_4$ cups arborio or carnaroli rice
5 cups chicken or vegetable stock,
   simmering
4 cooked beets (not in vinegar), diced
2 tbsp. chopped fresh dill

2 tbsp. fresh snipped chives
salt and pepper
$^2/_3$ cup freshly grated Parmesan
   cheese, to serve (optional)

1   Put the sour cherries in a saucepan with the wine and bring to a boil, then simmer for 2–3 minutes until slightly reduced. Remove from the heat and set aside.

2   Heat the olive oil in a large heavy-based saucepan over medium heat. Add the onion, celery, and thyme and cook for about 2 minutes until just beginning to soften. Add the garlic and rice and cook, stirring, until the rice is well coated.

3   Add a ladleful (about 1 cup) of the simmering stock; it will bubble and steam rapidly. Cook, stirring constantly, until the stock is absorbed.

4   Continue adding the stock, about half a ladleful at a time, allowing each addition to be absorbed before adding the next—never allow the rice to cook "dry." This should take 20–25 minutes. The risotto should have a creamy consistency and the rice

should be tender, but firm to the bite.

5   Halfway through the cooking time, remove the cherries from the wine with a slotted spoon and add to the risotto with the beets and half the wine. Continue adding the stock or remaining wine.

6   Stir in the dill and chives and season, if necessary. Serve with the Parmesan, if desired.

Zucchini & Basil Risotto

An easy way of livening up a simple risotto is to use a flavored olive oil—here a basil-flavored oil heightens the taste of the dish.

Serves 4–6

INGREDIENTS

4 tbsp. basil-flavored extra-virgin olive oil, plus extra for drizzling

4 zucchini, diced

1 yellow bell pepper, cored, deseeded, and diced

2 garlic cloves, finely chopped

1 large onion, finely chopped

2 cups arborio or carnaroli rice

⅓ cup dry white vermouth

6¼ cups chicken or vegetable stock, simmering

2 tbsp. unsalted butter, at room temperature

large handful of fresh basil leaves, torn, plus a few leaves to garnish

1 cup freshly grated Parmesan cheese

1 Heat half the oil in a large skillet over high heat. When very hot, but not smoking, add the zucchini and yellow bell pepper and stir-fry for 3 minutes until lightly golden. Stir in the garlic and cook for about 30 seconds longer. Transfer the zucchini and bell pepper to a plate and set aside.

2 Heat the remaining oil in a large heavy-based saucepan over medium heat. Add the chopped onion and cook for about 2 minutes until softened. Add the rice and cook, stirring frequently, for about 2 minutes until the rice is translucent and well coated with the oil.

3 Pour in the vermouth; it will bubble and steam rapidly and evaporate almost immediately. Add a ladleful (about 1 cup) of the simmering stock and cook, stirring constantly, until the stock is absorbed.

4 Continue adding the stock, about half a ladleful at a time, allowing each addition to be absorbed before adding the next. This should take 20–25 minutes. The risotto should have a creamy consistency and the rice should be tender, but still firm to the bite.

5 Stir in the zucchini mixture with any juices, the butter, basil, and Parmesan. Drizzle with a little oil and garnish with basil. Serve hot.

Wild Arugula & Tomato Risotto with Mozzarella

It's worth searching around for wild arugula as its robust peppery flavor makes all the difference to this dish. Teamed with vine-ripened plum tomatoes and real buffalo mozzarella, this risotto is sensational.

Serves 4–6

INGREDIENTS

2 tbsp. olive oil

2 tbsp. unsalted butter

1 large onion, finely chopped

2 garlic cloves, finely chopped

1¾ cups arborio rice

½ cup dry white vermouth (optional)

6¼ cups chicken or vegetable stock, simmering

6 vine-ripened or Italian plum tomatoes, deseeded and chopped

4½ oz. wild arugula

handful of fresh basil leaves

1⅓ cups freshly grated Parmesan cheese

8 oz. fresh Italian buffalo mozzarella, coarsely grated or diced

salt and pepper

1 Heat the oil and half the butter in a large skillet. Add the onion and cook for about 2 minutes until just beginning to soften. Stir in the garlic and rice and cook, stirring frequently, until the rice is translucent and well coated.

2 Pour in the white vermouth, if using; it will bubble and steam rapidly and evaporate almost immediately. Add a ladleful (about 1 cup) of the simmering stock and cook, stirring constantly, until it is absorbed.

3 Continue adding the stock, about half a ladleful at a time, allowing each addition to be absorbed before adding the next—never allow the rice to cook "dry."

4 Just before the rice is tender, stir in the chopped tomatoes and arugula. Shred the basil leaves and immediately stir into the risotto. Continue to cook, adding more stock, until the risotto is creamy and the rice is tender, but firm to the bite.

5 Remove from the heat and stir in the remaining butter, the Parmesan, and mozzarella. Season to taste with salt and pepper. Cover and stand for about 1 minute. Serve immediately, before the mozzarella melts completely.

Risotto with Sun-dried Tomatoes & Pecorino

Pecorino is an Italian cheese made from sheep's milk. Although it is made and used all over Italy, the aged pecorino from Sardinia—pecorino sardo—is particularly good for this dish.

Serves 6

INGREDIENTS

about 12 sun-dried tomatoes, not in oil

2 tbsp. olive oil

1 large onion, finely chopped

4–6 garlic cloves, finely chopped

2 cups arborio or carnaroli rice

6¼ cups chicken or vegetable stock, simmering

2 tbsp. chopped fresh flat-leaf parsley

1 cup grated aged pecorino cheese

extra-virgin olive oil, for drizzling

1 Place the sun-dried tomatoes in a bowl and pour over enough boiling water to cover. Stand for about 30 minutes until soft and supple. Drain and pat dry, then shred thinly and set aside.

2 Heat the oil in a heavy-based saucepan over medium heat. Add the onion and cook for about 2 minutes until beginning to soften. Add the garlic and cook for 15 seconds. Add the rice and cook, stirring frequently, for 2 minutes, until the rice is translucent and well coated with oil.

3 Add a ladleful (about 1 cup) of the hot stock; the stock will bubble and steam rapidly. Cook, stirring constantly, until the liquid is absorbed.

4 Continue adding the stock, about half a ladleful at a time, allowing each addition to be absorbed before adding the next—never allow the rice to cook "dry."

5 After about 15 minutes, stir in the sun-dried tomatoes. Continue to cook, adding the stock, until the rice is tender, but firm to the bite. The risotto should have a creamy consistency.

6 Remove from the heat and stir in the parsley and half the cheese. Cover, stand for about 1 minute, then spoon into serving dishes. Drizzle with extra-virgin olive oil and sprinkle the remaining cheese over the top. Serve immediately.

Orange-scented Risotto

This fragrant risotto makes a delicate first course for a special meal.
Serve with a sprinkling of grated Parmesan, if desired.

Serves 4

INGREDIENTS

2 tbsp. pine nuts
4 tbsp. unsalted butter
2 shallots, finely chopped
1 leek, finely shredded

2 cups arborio or carnaroli rice
2 tbsp. orange-flavored liqueur or dry
  white vermouth
6¼ cups chicken or vegetable stock,
  simmering

grated rind of 1 orange
juice of 2 oranges, strained
3 tbsp. snipped fresh chives
salt and pepper

1 Toast the pine nuts in a skillet over medium heat for about 3 minutes, stirring and shaking frequently, until golden brown. Set aside.

2 Heat half the butter in a large heavy-based saucepan over medium heat. Add the shallots and leek and cook for about 2 minutes until they begin to soften. Add the rice and cook, stirring frequently, for about 2 minutes, until the rice is translucent and well coated with the butter.

3 Pour in the liqueur or vermouth; it will bubble and steam rapidly and evaporate almost immediately. Add a ladleful (about 1 cup) of the hot stock and cook, stirring, until absorbed.

4 Continue adding the stock, about half a ladleful at a time, allowing each addition to be absorbed before adding the next—never allow the rice to cook "dry."

5 After about 15 minutes, add the orange rind and juice and continue to cook, adding more

stock, until the rice is tender, but firm to the bite. The risotto should have a creamy consistency.

6 Remove from the heat and stir in the remaining butter and 2 tablespoons of the chives. Season with salt and pepper. Spoon into serving dishes and sprinkle with the toasted pine nuts and the remaining chives.

Black Cherry Risotto

This risotto is flavored like a rice pilaf, using cherries and almonds.
It has a delicious fruity yet tangy flavor.

Serves 6

INGREDIENTS

2 tbsp. unblanched almonds

2 tbsp. sunflower or vegetable oil

1 red onion, finely chopped

2 tbsp. dried sour cherries or raisins

1 lb. black cherries or small black
plums, pitted and halved

1¾ cups arborio or carnaroli rice

1 cup port or fruity red wine

5 cups chicken or vegetable stock,
simmering

¼ cup heavy cream (optional)

2 tbsp. chopped fresh chives, plus
whole chives for garnishing

salt and pepper

1 Lightly toast the almonds in a skillet for about 2 minutes until golden. Cool, then chop coarsely. Set aside.

2 Heat the oil in a large heavy-based saucepan over medium heat. Add the onion and cook, stirring frequently, for about 2 minutes until beginning to soften. Add the dried cherries and the black cherries and stir for 2–3 minutes until the cherries begin to soften. Add the rice to the pan and cook, stirring frequently, until the rice is translucent and well coated.

3 Pour in the port; it will bubble and steam rapidly. Cook, stirring, until it is absorbed. Add a ladleful (about 1 cup) of the simmering stock and cook, stirring constantly until the stock is absorbed.

4 Continue adding the stock, about half a ladleful at a time, allowing each addition to be absorbed before adding the next—

never allow the rice to cook "dry." This should take 20–25 minutes. The risotto should have a creamy consistency and the rice should be tender, but still firm to the bite.

5 Stir in the cream, if using, and season with salt and pepper. Remove from the heat, stir in the chives, and spoon into serving bowls. Sprinkle with the chopped almonds, garnish with the chives, and serve immediately.

Crab Risotto with Roasted Bell Peppers

A different way to make the most of crab,
this rich-tasting and colorful risotto is full of interesting flavors.

Serves 4–6

INGREDIENTS

2–3 large red bell peppers
3 tbsp. olive oil
1 onion, finely chopped
1 small fennel bulb, finely chopped
2 stalks celery, finely chopped
¼–½ tsp. cayenne pepper, or to taste

1¾ cups arborio or carnaroli rice
1 lb. 12 oz. can Italian peeled plum
  tomatoes, drained and chopped
¼ cup dry white vermouth (optional)
6¼ cups fish or light chicken stock,
  simmering
1 lb. fresh cooked crab meat (white
  and dark meat)

¼ cup lemon juice
2–4 tbsp. chopped fresh parsley or
  chervil
salt and pepper

1 Broil the bell peppers until the skins are charred. Transfer to a plastic bag and twist to seal. When cool enough to handle, peel off the charred skins, working over a bowl to catch the juices. Remove the cores and seeds; chop the flesh and set aside, reserving the juices.

2 Heat the olive oil in a large heavy-based saucepan. Add the onion, fennel, and celery and cook for 2–3 minutes until the vegetables are softened. Add the cayenne and rice and cook, stirring frequently, for about 2 minutes until the rice is translucent and well coated.

3 Stir in the tomatoes and vermouth, if using. The liquid will bubble and steam rapidly. When the liquid is almost absorbed, add a ladleful (about 1 cup) of the simmering stock. Cook, stirring constantly, until the liquid is completely absorbed.

4 Continue adding the stock, about half a ladleful at a time, allowing each addition to be absorbed before adding the next. This should take 20–25 minutes. The risotto should have a creamy consistency and the rice should be tender, but firm to the bite.

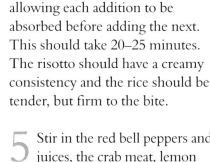

5 Stir in the red bell peppers and juices, the crab meat, lemon juice, and parsley or chervil, and heat. Season with salt and pepper to taste. Serve immediately.

Risotto with Clams

This simple recipe is an excellent way of using the tiny Venus clams when they are in season. The tomatoes add a splash of color.

Serves 6

INGREDIENTS

1/4 cup olive oil
1 large onion, finely chopped
4 lb. 8 oz. tiny clams, such as Venus, well scrubbed
1/2 cup dry white wine
4 cups fish stock

2 1/2 cups water
3 garlic cloves, finely chopped
1/2 tsp. crushed dried chili (or to taste)
2 cups arborio or carnaroli rice
3 ripe plum tomatoes, skinned and coarsely chopped

3 tbsp. lemon juice
2 tbsp. chopped fresh chervil or parsley
salt and pepper

1 Heat 1–2 tablespoons of the oil in a large heavy-based saucepan over medium-high heat. Add the onion and stir-fry for about 1 minute. Add the clams and wine and cover tightly. Cook for 2–3 minutes, shaking the pan frequently, until the clams begin to open. Remove from the heat and discard any clams that do not open.

2 When cool enough to handle, remove the clams from their shells. Rinse in the cooking liquid. Cover the clams and set aside.

Strain the cooking liquid through a paper coffee filter or a sieve lined with a paper towel, and reserve.

3 Bring the fish stock and water to a boil in a saucepan, then reduce the heat and keep at a gentle simmer.

4 Heat the remaining olive oil in a large, heavy-based saucepan over medium heat. Add the garlic and chili and cook gently for 1 minute. Add the rice and cook, stirring frequently, for about

2 minutes until translucent and well coated with oil.

5 Add a ladleful (about 1 cup) of the simmering stock mixture; it will bubble and steam rapidly. Cook, stirring constantly, until the liquid is completely absorbed.

6 Continue adding the stock, about half a ladleful at a time, allowing each addition to be absorbed before adding the next—never allow the rice to cook "dry." This should take 20–25 minutes. The risotto should have a creamy consistency and the rice should be tender, but firm to the bite.

7 Stir in the tomatoes, reserved clams and their cooking liquid, the lemon juice, and chervil. Heat through. Season to taste and serve immediately.

Black Risotto

This classic recipe gets its name from the squid ink, which turns the risotto "black." A sophisticated dish, sure to impress.

Serves 6

INGREDIENTS

2–3 tbsp. olive oil

1 lb. cleaned squid or cuttlefish, cut crosswise into thin strips, rinsed, and patted dry

2 tbsp. lemon juice

2 tbsp. unsalted butter

3–4 garlic cloves, finely chopped

1 tsp. crushed dried chili, or to taste

1¾ cups arborio or carnaroli rice

½ cup dry white wine

4 cups fish stock, simmering

2 tbsp. squid or cuttlefish ink

2 tbsp. chopped fresh flat-leaf parsley

salt and pepper

1 Heat half the olive oil in a large heavy-based skillet over medium-high heat. When the oil is very hot, add the squid strips and stir-fry for 2–3 minutes until just cooked. Transfer to a plate and sprinkle with the lemon juice.

2 Heat the remaining olive oil and butter in a large heavy-based pan over medium heat. Add the garlic and chili and cook gently for 1 minute. Add the rice and cook, stirring frequently,

for about 2 minutes until translucent and well coated.

3 Pour in the white wine; it will bubble and steam rapidly. Cook, stirring frequently, until the wine is completely absorbed by the rice. Add a ladleful (about 1 cup) of the simmering fish stock and cook, stirring constantly, until it is completely absorbed.

4 Continue adding the stock, about half a ladleful at a time, allowing each addition to be

absorbed before adding the next—never allow the rice to cook "dry." This should take 20–25 minutes. The risotto should have a creamy consistency and the rice should be tender, but firm to the bite.

5 Just before adding the last ladleful of stock, add the squid ink to the stock and stir to blend completely. Stir into the risotto with the reserved squid pieces and the parsley. Season with salt and pepper to taste. Serve immediately.

Rich Lobster Risotto

Although lobster is expensive, this dish is worth it.
Keeping it simple allows the lobster flavor to come through.

Serves 4

INGREDIENTS

1 tbsp. vegetable oil
4 tbsp. unsalted butter
2 shallots, finely chopped
1½ cups arborio or carnaroli rice
½ tsp. cayenne pepper, or to taste

⅓ cup dry white vermouth
6¼ cups shellfish, fish, or light
   chicken stock, simmering
8 oz. cherry tomatoes, quartered and
   deseeded

2–3 tbsp. heavy or whipping cream
about 2 cups cooked lobster meat, cut
   into coarse chunks
2 tbsp. chopped fresh chervil or dill
salt and white pepper

1 Heat the oil and half the butter in a large heavy-based saucepan over medium heat. Add the shallots and cook for about 2 minutes until just beginning to soften. Add the rice and cayenne pepper and cook, stirring frequently, for about 2 minutes, until the rice is translucent and well coated with the oil and butter.

2 Pour in the vermouth; it will bubble and steam rapidly and evaporate almost immediately.

Add a ladleful (about 1 cup) of the simmering stock and cook, stirring constantly, until the stock is absorbed.

3 Continue adding the stock, about half a ladleful at a time, allowing each addition to be absorbed before adding the next—never allow the rice to cook "dry." This should take 20–25 minutes. The risotto should have a creamy consistency and the rice should be tender, but firm to the bite.

4 Stir in the tomatoes and cream and cook for about 2 minutes.

5 Add the cooked lobster meat, with the remaining butter and chervil, and cook long enough to just heat the lobster meat gently. Serve immediately.

Radicchio Risotto with Pancetta & Cream

*In this risotto, the slightly bitter flavor of radicchio is balanced by the
addition of sweet heavy cream, while pancetta provides a subtle smoky contrast.*

Serves 6–8

INGREDIENTS

1 large head radicchio, outer damaged
  leaves removed
2 tbsp. sunflower or other
  vegetable oil
2 tbsp. unsalted butter
4 oz. pancetta or thick-cut smoky
  bacon, diced

1 large onion, finely chopped
1 garlic clove, finely chopped
2 cups arborio or carnaroli rice
6¼ cups chicken or vegetable stock,
  simmering
¼ cup heavy cream
⅔ cup freshly grated Parmesan cheese

3–4 tbsp. chopped fresh flat-leaf
  parsley
salt and pepper
fresh flat-leaf parsley sprigs, to
  garnish

1 Cut the radicchio head in half lengthwise; remove the triangular core. Place the halves cut-side down and shred finely. Set aside.

2 Heat the oil and butter in a heavy-based pan over medium-high heat. Add the diced pancetta and cook for 3–4 minutes, stirring occasionally, until it begins to color. Add the onion and garlic and cook for 1 minute, or until just beginning to soften.

3 Add the rice and cook, stirring frequently, for 2 minutes, until translucent and well coated with the oil and butter. Stir in the radicchio for 1 minute until just beginning to wilt. Reduce the heat to medium.

4 Add a ladleful (about 1 cup) of the simmering stock; the stock will bubble and steam rapidly. Cook, stirring constantly, until the stock is completely absorbed.

5 Continue adding the stock, about half a ladleful at a time, allowing each addition to be absorbed before adding the next. This should take 20–25 minutes. The risotto should have a creamy consistency and the rice should be tender, but firm to the bite.

6 Stir in the cream, Parmesan, and parsley. Season with salt and pepper. Remove from the heat. Cover and let stand for 1 minute. Garnish with parsley and serve.

Italian Sausage & Rosemary Risotto

This recipe is made with a mild Italian sausage called luganega, *but you can use any sausage you like—
sweet fennel sausage, a very spicy Italian sausage, or even a Spanish chorizo would produce a good result.*

Serves 4–6

INGREDIENTS

2 long sprigs fresh rosemary, plus
   extra to garnish

2 tbsp. olive oil

4 tbsp. unsalted butter

1 large onion, finely chopped

1 stalk celery, finely chopped

2 garlic cloves, finely chopped

$\frac{1}{2}$ tsp. dried thyme leaves

1 lb. pork sausage such as *luganega* or
   Cumberland, cut into $\frac{1}{2}$-inch pieces

$1\frac{3}{4}$ cups arborio or carnaroli rice

$\frac{1}{2}$ cup fruity red wine

$5\frac{2}{3}$ cups chicken stock, simmering

1 cup freshly grated Parmesan cheese

salt and pepper

1 Strip the long thin leaves from the rosemary sprigs and chop finely; set aside.

2 Heat the oil and half the butter in a large heavy-based saucepan over medium heat. Add the onion and celery and cook for about 2 minutes. Stir in the garlic, thyme, sausage, and rosemary. Cook for about 5 minutes, stirring frequently, until the sausage begins to brown. Transfer the sausage to a plate.

3 Stir the rice into the pan and cook for about 2 minutes until the grains are translucent and coated with the butter and oil.

4 Pour in the red wine; it will bubble and steam rapidly and evaporate almost immediately. Add a ladleful (about 1 cup) of the simmering stock and cook, stirring, until it is absorbed.

5 Continue adding the stock, about half a ladleful at a time, allowing each addition to be absorbed before adding the next. This should take 20–25 minutes. The risotto should have a creamy consistency and the rice should be tender, but firm to the bite.

6 Return the sausage pieces to the risotto and heat through. Remove from the heat; stir in the remaining butter and Parmesan. Season with salt and pepper. Cover, let stand for about 1 minute, then garnish with rosemary. Serve.

Arrancini

These little risotto-ball snacks are as popular in New York as they are in Rome.
The mozzarella centers ooze deliciously when you bite into them.

Serves 6–8

INGREDIENTS

1 quantity Easy Cheesy Risotto
   with Parmesan (see page 100),
   completely cooled
3 eggs
3 tbsp. chopped fresh flat-leaf parsley

²/₃ cup mozzarella, diced
vegetable oil, for frying
about ²/₃ cup all-purpose flour

about 1¹/₂ cups dried breadcrumbs,
   preferably homemade
salt and pepper

1 Put the risotto in a large mixing bowl and stir to break up. Beat 2 of the eggs lightly, then gradually beat enough into the risotto until the risotto begins to stick together. Beat in the parsley.

2 Using wet hands, form the mixture into balls about the size of a large egg.

3 Poke a hole in the center of each ball and fill with a few cubes of the mozzarella. Carefully seal the hole over with the risotto mixture. Place on a large cookie sheet.

4 In a deep-fat fryer or large heavy-based saucepan, heat about 3 inches of oil to 350-375°F or until a cube of bread browns.

5 Spread the flour on a large plate and season with salt and pepper. In a small bowl, beat the remaining egg and add any unused egg from Step 1. Spread the breadcrumbs on another large plate and season with salt and pepper.

6 Roll each risotto ball in a little seasoned flour, shaking off the excess. Carefully coat in the egg,

then roll in the breadcrumbs to coat completely.

7 Deep fry 3–4 balls for about 2 minutes until crisp and golden, then transfer to paper towels to drain. Keep hot in a warm oven while frying the remaining balls. Serve immediately while the cheese is still soft and melted.

Frittata Risotto

An excellent way of using up leftover risotto, this fried risotto "cake" makes a great first course, or a tasty accompaniment to roasted or broiled meats.

Serves 4–6

INGREDIENTS

about ⅓ cup olive oil

1 large red onion, finely chopped

1 red bell pepper, cored, deseeded, and chopped

1 garlic clove, finely chopped

3–4 sun-dried tomatoes, finely shredded

2 tbsp. chopped fresh flat-leaf parsley or basil

1 quantity Easy Cheesy Risotto with Parmesan (see page 100) or Risotto alla Milanese (see page 156), cooled

about ⅔ cup freshly grated Parmesan cheese

1 Heat 2 tablespoons of the oil in a large heavy-based skillet over medium-high heat. Add the onion and red bell pepper and cook for 3–4 minutes until the vegetables are soft.

2 Add the garlic and sun-dried tomatoes and cook for 2 minutes. Remove from the heat. Stir in the parsley; cool slightly.

3 Put the risotto in a bowl and break up with a fork. Stir in the vegetable mixture with half the Parmesan. Stir to mix well.

4 Reserve 1 tablespoon of the remaining oil and heat the rest in the cleaned skillet over medium heat. Remove from the heat and spoon in the risotto mixture, pressing it into an even cake-like layer, about ¾–1 inch thick. Return to the heat and cook for about 4 minutes until crisp and brown on the bottom.

5 With a palette knife, loosen the edges and give the pan a shake. Slide the frittata onto a large plate. Protecting your hands, invert the skillet over the frittata

and, holding both firmly together, flip them over. Return to the heat and drizzle the remaining oil around the edge of the frittata, gently pulling the edges toward the center with the palette knife. Cook for 1–2 minutes to seal the bottom, then slide onto a serving plate.

6 Sprinkle the top with some of the remaining Parmesan. Cut into wedges and serve with the rest of the Parmesan.

Cheese-topped Risotto Tart with Spinach

Risotto, combined with spinach and cheese, makes a mouthwatering filling for this tart. If preferred, you can use six 4-inch individual tart tins instead of a large one.

Serves 6–8

INGREDIENTS

1²/₃ cups all-purpose flour
¹/₂ tsp. salt
1 tsp. superfine sugar
¹/₂ cup unsalted butter, diced
1 egg yolk, beaten with 2 tbsp. iced
  water

FILLING:
1 quantity Easy Cheesy Risotto with
  Parmesan (see page 100), still warm
9 oz. spinach, cooked, drained very
  well, and chopped
2 tbsp. heavy cream

8 oz. mozzarella, preferably buffalo
1 cup freshly grated Parmesan cheese

1 To make the shortcrust pastry, sift the flour, salt, and sugar into a large bowl and sprinkle the butter over. Rub the butter into the flour until the mixture forms coarse crumbs. Sprinkle in the egg mixture and stir to make a dough.

2 Gather the dough into a ball, wrap in plastic wrap, and chill for at least 1 hour.

3 Gently roll out the pastry to a thickness of about ⅛ inch, then use to line a lightly greased 9–10 inch tart tin with a removable base. Prick the bottom with a fork and chill for 1 hour.

4 Cover the tart case with waxed paper and fill with baking beans. Bake in a preheated oven at 400°F for about 20 minutes until the pastry is set and the edge is golden. Remove the beans and waxed paper and set aside. Reduce the oven temperature to 350°F.

5 Put the risotto in a bowl and stir in the spinach, cream, half the mozzarella, and half the Parmesan. Spoon into the tart case and smooth the top. Sprinkle evenly with the remaining cheeses.

6 Bake for 12–15 minutes or until cooked through and golden. Cool slightly on a wire rack, then serve warm.

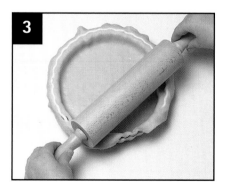

Oven-baked Risotto with Mushrooms

This easy-to-make risotto is a good choice for entertaining as it eliminates the need for constant stirring. The result is creamy and moist—more like a rice pudding.

Serves 4–6

INGREDIENTS

4 tbsp. olive oil
14 oz. portobello or large field
  mushrooms, thickly sliced
4 oz. pancetta or thick-cut smoky
  bacon, diced
1 large onion, finely chopped

2 garlic cloves, finely chopped
1¾ cups arborio or carnaroli rice
5 cups chicken stock, simmering
2 tbsp. chopped fresh tarragon or flat-
  leaf parsley

1 cup freshly grated Parmesan cheese,
  plus extra for sprinkling
salt and pepper

1 Heat 2 tablespoons of the oil in a large heavy-based skillet over high heat. Add the mushrooms and stir-fry for 2–3 minutes until golden and tender-crisp. Transfer to a plate.

2 Add the pancetta to the pan and cook for about 2 minutes, stirring frequently, until crisp and golden. Add to the mushrooms on the plate.

3 Heat the remaining oil in a heavy-based saucepan over

medium heat. Add the onion and cook for about 2 minutes until beginning to soften. Add the garlic and rice and cook, stirring, for about 2 minutes until the rice is well coated with the oil.

4 Gradually stir the stock into the rice, then add the mushroom and pancetta mixture and the tarragon. Season with salt and pepper. Bring to a boil.

5 Remove from the heat and transfer to a casserole.

6 Cover and bake in a preheated oven at 350°F for about 20 minutes until the rice is almost tender and most of the liquid is absorbed. Uncover and stir in the Parmesan. Continue to bake for about 15 minutes longer until the rice is tender, but still firm to the bite. Serve at once with extra Parmesan for sprinkling.

Famous Rice Dishes

In this chapter, you can travel the world and sample some of the traditional and delectable rice dishes that have evolved in the various rice-producing countries over hundreds of years, using a blend of exotic flavors and ingredients.

For a flavor of Europe, try your hand at making a Spanish Paella, a wonderful mix of chicken, shellfish, and rice; or serve the delicately flavored Greek Egg & Lemon Soup as a light lunch. Traveling to the Middle East, savor an unusual, spicy lamb and rice sausage, Mumbar; or learn how to make delicious Mujadarah, a marvelous combination of rice, lentils, and caramelized onions.

Capture the exotic flavors of India with Murgh Pullau, a fragrant chicken and almond pilaf, or discover the delights of Thai cooking with spicy red pork curry with jasmine-scented rice. Popular Chinese Fried Rice is a must to try at home, and the classic fried rice dish of Indonesia, Nasi Goreng, a medley of Far-Eastern flavors, is ideal for any occasion. Vietnamese Spring Rolls are a culinary treat and fun to eat, while for entertaining, Japanese Sushi make stunning fare.

Risotto alla Milanese

This risotto, traditionally served as an accompaniment to Ossobuco alla Milanese, is one of the world's most beautiful and elegant dishes.

Serves 4–6

INGREDIENTS

¹/₂–1 tsp. saffron threads
5²/₃ cups chicken stock, simmering
6 tbsp. unsalted butter
2–3 shallots, finely chopped

2 cups arborio or carnaroli rice
2 cups freshly grated Parmesan cheese
salt and pepper

1 Put the saffron threads in a small bowl. Pour enough of the stock over to cover the threads, then set aside to infuse.

2 Melt 2 tablespoons of the butter in a large heavy-based pan over medium heat. Add the shallots and cook for about 2 minutes until beginning to soften. Add the rice and cook, stirring frequently, for about 2 minutes, until the rice is beginning to turn translucent and is well coated.

3 Add a ladleful (about 1 cup) of the simmering stock; it will steam and bubble rapidly. Cook, stirring constantly, until the liquid is absorbed.

4 Continue adding the stock, about half a ladleful at a time, allowing each addition to be absorbed before adding the next—never allow the rice to cook "dry."

5 After about 15 minutes, stir in the saffron-infused stock; the rice will turn a vibrant yellow and the color will become deeper as it cooks. Continue cooking, adding the stock in the same way until the rice is tender, but still firm to the bite. The risotto should have a creamy porridge-like consistency.

6 Stir in the remaining butter and half the Parmesan, then remove from the heat. Cover and let stand for about 1 minute.

7 Spoon the risotto into serving bowls and serve immediately with the remaining Parmesan.

Dolmades

These stuffed grape leaves are popular all over the Middle-East, where they are served as part of a meze—a selection of appetizers. This is a simple rice version.

Serves 10–12

INGREDIENTS

about 24 large grape leaves, packed in
  brine, drained
olive oil
1 onion, finely chopped
2 garlic cloves, finely chopped
³/₄ tsp. dried thyme
³/₄ tsp. dried oregano

¹/₂ tsp. ground cinnamon
1 cup long-grain white rice
1¹/₂ cups water
2 tsp. raisins
2 tbsp. pine nuts, lightly toasted
2 tbsp. chopped fresh mint
1 tbsp. chopped fresh flat-leaf parsley

4 tbsp. lemon juice
1¹/₂ cups chicken stock
salt and pepper

1 Cover the grape leaves with boiling water and let stand for 2 minutes. Drain, rinse, and pat dry. Cut off any thick stems. Place shiny-side down on paper towels.

2 Heat 2 tablespoons of the olive oil in a heavy-based pan. Add the onion and cook for about 3 minutes until soft. Stir in the garlic, dried herbs, and cinnamon, then add the rice and cook for about 2 minutes, stirring, until translucent and coated with the oil.

3 Stir in the water and raisins and bring to a boil, stirring twice. Simmer, covered tightly, for 15 minutes until the liquid is absorbed and the rice just tender.

4 Fork the rice into a bowl and add the pine nuts, mint, parsley, and half the lemon juice. Stir and season with salt and pepper and 1 tablespoon olive oil.

5 Place about 1 tablespoon of the rice mixture on a grape leaf near the stem end and roll the leaf once over the filling. Fold in each side of the leaf; finish rolling. Repeat with the remaining leaves.

6 Brush a large deep flameproof dish or casserole with about 2 tablespoons of olive oil. Arrange the dolmades tightly in 2 rows, making a second layer if necessary. Sprinkle with another tablespoon of the oil and the remaining lemon juice. Add the stock to cover the rolls; add extra water if necessary to make enough liquid.

7 Weight down the rolls with a heatproof plate, cover tightly with a lid or kitchen foil, and cook over very low heat for about 1 hour. Remove from the heat and allow to cool to room temperature. Drain and serve with a little of the cooking juices, if desired.

Mujadarah

This delicious combination of rice, lentils, and caramelized onions
is often served as part of a Lebanese meze.

Serves 6

INGREDIENTS

1 cup green or brown lentils, rinsed
½ cup olive oil
3 large onions, thinly sliced
1 cup basmati or long-grain white rice

3 cups light chicken or vegetable
  stock
1 tsp. ground allspice or ground
  cinnamon
salt and pepper

TO SERVE:
lemon wedges
scallions, thinly sliced on the diagonal
natural yogurt

1 Bring a large saucepan of water to a boil. Pour in the lentils gradually, so the water remains boiling. Reduce the heat to medium-low and simmer for about 25 minutes, skimming off any foam that rises to the surface, until just tender. Drain the lentils and set aside (see Cook's Tip).

2 Meanwhile, heat the oil in a large, deep skillet over medium heat until very hot. Add the onions and cook for 4–5 minutes until soft. Using a slotted spoon, transfer about two-thirds of the onions to a bowl; set aside. Continue cooking the remaining onions until brown and crisp, then drain on a paper towel.

3 Add the rice to the pan and cook, stirring frequently, for about 2 minutes until translucent and well coated with the oil. Add the less-cooked onions, with the lentils and stock, and stir gently, scraping the base of the pan to release any crispy bits. Add the ground allspice and season with salt and pepper.

4 Tightly cover the pan and cook over very low heat for about 20 minutes until the rice is tender and all the stock is absorbed. Fork the rice mixture into a serving bowl; top with the crispy onions. Serve with lemon wedges, scallions, and yogurt.

COOK'S TIP

If preferred, reserve the lentil
cooking liquid and use instead of
the chicken or vegetable stock.

Greek Egg & Lemon Soup

The rice not only adds texture to this soup, but also helps to thicken the broth slightly.
Add the egg and lemon mixture carefully as the soup can easily curdle.

Serves 6–8

INGREDIENTS

6¼ cups chicken or lamb stock
⅓–½ cup long-grain white rice
3 eggs, separated
3–4 tbsp. lemon juice

1 tbsp. water
salt and white pepper
1 tbsp. chopped fresh flat-leaf
    parsley, to garnish (optional)

1 Bring the stock to a boil in a large saucepan. Add the rice in a very slow stream so the stock does not stop boiling; stir once or twice. Reduce the heat and simmer gently, partially covered, until the rice is tender; skim off any foam that rises to the surface.

2 Whisk the egg whites in a large bowl until almost stiff.

3 Add the egg yolks and continue whisking until the mixture is light and creamy. Gradually beat in the lemon juice and water.

4 Gradually whisk in half of the hot stock and rice, about 2 tablespoons at a time. Be careful to add the hot stock very slowly to the egg and lemon mixture, and whisk constantly; otherwise the eggs may curdle.

5 Remove the remaining stock and rice from the heat, transfer to a bowl, and gradually whisk in the egg and stock mixture. Continue to whisk for 1 minute to allow the stock to cool slightly. Season with salt and pepper and serve immediately. Garnish with a little chopped parsley, if desired.

COOK'S TIP

Using a food processor can help prevent the egg and lemon mixture from curdling. Add the egg whites to a food processor fitted with the metal blade and process for about 1 minute until very thick and foamy. Add the egg yolks and continue to process for 1 minute. With the machine running, gradually pour the lemon and water through the feed tube until combined. Continue from Step 4.

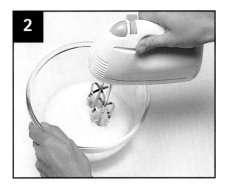

Kedgeree

Originally served at Victorian breakfast tables, kedgeree probably derives from an Indian dish called khichri. The strong flavor of the smoked fish is a perfect match for the blandness of rice.

Serves 4–6

INGREDIENTS

1½ lb. thick, undyed smoked haddock or cod fillets
milk, for poaching
2 bay leaves
1 tbsp. vegetable oil
4 tbsp. butter
1 onion, finely chopped

1 tsp. hot curry powder, or to taste
1 tsp. dry mustard powder
1½ cups basmati rice
3½ cups water
2 small leeks, trimmed and cut into ¼-inch slices

2 tbsp. chopped fresh flat-leaf parsley or cilantro
a squeeze of lemon juice
3–4 hard-boiled (hard-cooked) eggs, peeled and quartered
salt and pepper
lemon quarters, to serve

1 Put the fish in a skillet and pour in enough milk to just cover; add the bay leaves. Bring to a boil, then simmer gently, covered, for about 4 minutes. Remove from the heat and let stand, covered, for about 10 minutes.

2 Using a slotted spoon, transfer the fish to a plate and cover loosely; set aside. Reserve the cooking milk, discarding the bay leaves.

3 Heat the oil and half the butter in a large pan over medium heat. Add the onion and cook for about 2 minutes until soft. Stir in the curry powder and the mustard powder and cook for 1 minute.

4 Add the rice and stir for about 2 minutes until well coated. Add the water and bring to a boil; stir and reduce the heat to very low. Cook, covered, for 20–25 minutes until the rice is tender and the water absorbed.

5 Melt the remaining butter in a flameproof casserole, add the leeks, and cook for about 4 minutes until soft. Fork the leeks into the hot rice. Add 2–3 tablespoons of the reserved milk to moisten.

6 Flake the fish off the skin into large pieces and fold into the rice. Stir in the parsley and lemon juice, then season with salt and pepper. Add a little more milk, if desired, then add the egg quarters. Serve, with lemon quarters.

Spanish Paella

*This classic recipe gets its name from the wide metal pan
traditionally used for cooking the dish—a paellera.*

Serves 4

INGREDIENTS

½ cup olive oil

3 lb. 5 oz. chicken, cut into
   8 pieces

12 oz. chorizo sausage, cut into
   ½-inch pieces

4 oz. cured ham, chopped

2 onions, finely chopped

2 red bell peppers, cored, deseeded,
   and cut into 1-inch pieces

4–6 garlic cloves

3¾ cups short-grain Spanish rice or
   Italian arborio rice

2 bay leaves

1 tsp. dried thyme

1 tsp. saffron threads, lightly crushed

1 cup dry white wine

6¼ cups chicken stock

4 oz. fresh shelled or defrosted
   frozen peas

1 lb. medium uncooked shrimp

8 raw King shrimp, in shells

16 clams, very well scrubbed

16 mussels, very well scrubbed

salt and pepper

4 tbsp. chopped fresh flat-leaf
   parsley

1 Heat half the oil in a 18-inch paella pan or deep, wide skillet over medium-high heat. Add the chicken and fry gently, turning, until golden brown. Remove from the pan and set aside.

2 Add the chorizo and ham to the pan and cook for about 7 minutes, stirring occasionally, until crisp. Remove and set aside.

3 Stir the onions into the pan and cook for about 3 minutes until soft. Add the bell peppers and garlic and cook until beginning to soften; remove and set aside.

4 Add the remaining oil to the pan and stir in the rice until well coated. Add the bay leaves, thyme, and saffron and stir well. Pour in the wine, simmer, then pour in the stock, stirring well and

scraping the bottom of the pan. Bring to a boil, stirring often.

5 Stir in the cooked vegetables. Add the chorizo, ham, and chicken and gently bury in the rice. Reduce the heat and cook for 10 minutes, stirring occasionally.

6 Add the peas and shrimp and cook for a further 5 minutes. Push the clams and mussels into the rice. Cover and cook over very low heat for about 5 minutes until the rice is tender and the shellfish open. Discard any unopened clams or mussels. Season to taste.

7 Remove from heat and let stand, covered, for about 5 minutes. Sprinkle with parsley and serve.

Salmon Coulibiac

Coulibiac is probably the world's best fish pie. It was first made in the 19th century by French chefs working in the Imperial Russian courts.

Serves 6–8

INGREDIENTS

8 tbsp. butter, plus extra 2 tbsp. butter, melted

2 onions, finely chopped

generous ½ cup long-grain white rice

1 lb. 10 oz. skinned salmon fillet, poached in water, cooking liquid reserved

5½ oz. mushrooms, thinly sliced

3 oz. cooked spinach, chopped

2 tbsp. chopped fresh dill

6 canned anchovy fillets in oil, drained and chopped

5 hard-boiled eggs, coarsely chopped

grated rind and juice of 1 large lemon

12½ oz. packet puff pastry

1 egg, beaten, for glaze

salt and pepper

lemon wedges and dill sprigs, to garnish

1 Melt half of the butter in a large saucepan, add half the onion, and cook for about 2 minutes until soft. Stir in the rice for 2 minutes until well coated.

2 If necessary, add water to the reserved fish cooking liquid to make up to 1 cup. Add to the rice, bring to a boil, then cover and cook very gently for about 18 minutes. Allow to cool.

3 Melt the remaining butter in a skillet, add the remaining onions and mushrooms, and cook for about 8 minutes until there is no liquid. Add the spinach and dill. Season well, then cool.

4 Add the anchovies, eggs, and lemon rind and juice to the mushroom mixture and toss well.

5 Roll out the puff pastry and cut into two squares, one

11 inches square and the other 12 inches square. Place the smaller piece on a lightly greased cookie sheet and spread half the mushroom mixture over, leaving a 1-inch border; spoon half the rice over.

6 Center the salmon on top of the rice layer and cover with the remaining rice. Spoon the remaining mushroom mixture over. Drizzle the melted butter over the top. Brush the pastry edges with egg, cover with the second square, and seal the edges.

7 Brush with egg and mark a lattice pattern on top. Bake in a preheated oven 425°F for about 35 minutes until golden. Rest on a wire rack, then serve garnished.

Stuffed Cabbage

Hailing from Eastern Europe, this recipe is a delicious way to stretch a small amount of meat.
Use the smaller cabbage leaves too—simply overlap them to create the size of the larger leaves.

Serves 6–8

INGREDIENTS

1 cup fresh white breadcrumbs
½ cup milk
1 tbsp. vegetable oil
1 onion, finely chopped
2 garlic cloves, finely chopped
1 lb. ground beef
1 lb. ground pork or veal
2 tbsp. tomato ketchup
3 tbsp. chopped fresh dill
1 tsp. chopped fresh thyme leaves

½ cup long-grain white rice
salt and pepper
1 large cabbage, such as Savoy, leaves
    separated and blanched

TOMATO SAUCE:
2 large onions, thinly sliced
2 tbsp. olive oil
2 x 14 oz. cans chopped tomatoes
2 cups strained tomatoes or tomato
    sauce

¼ cup tomato ketchup
grated rind and juice of 1 large lemon
2 tbsp. light brown sugar
2¾ oz. raisins

1 Combine the breadcrumbs and the milk; let soak. Cook the onion and garlic in the oil for about 2 minutes until soft, then set aside.

2 Place the beef and pork or veal in a bowl. Mix in the ketchup, herbs, rice, and seasoning. Add the breadcrumbs, cooked onion, and garlic.

3 To make the tomato sauce, cook the onions in the oil for 3 minutes until soft. Stir in the tomatoes and the remaining ingredients and bring to a boil, then simmer for about 15 minutes, stirring occasionally. Set aside.

4 To fill the leaves, spoon 1–2 tablespoons of the meat mixture onto a cabbage leaf above the stem end. Fold the stem end over the filling, then fold over the sides. Roll up to enclose. Repeat with the remaining leaves.

5 Spoon enough tomato sauce to cover the base of a large baking dish. Arrange the filled cabbage rolls, seam-side down, in the dish. Spoon the remaining sauce over the rolls to just cover— add a little water if necessary. Cover tightly and bake in a preheated oven at 325°F for about 1½ hours, basting once or twice.

6 Transfer the cabbage rolls to a serving plate and keep warm. Simmer the sauce to thicken, if necessary. Serve at once.

Mediterranean Stuffed Peppers

Serve the bell peppers with their tops for an attractive finish—blanch them with the peppers, then bake separately for the last 10 minutes and place in position just before serving.

Serves 6

INGREDIENTS

6 large bell peppers, red, yellow, and orange
1 cup long-grain white rice
2–3 tbsp. olive oil, plus extra for greasing and drizzling
1 large onion
2 stalks celery, chopped

2 garlic cloves, finely chopped
$\frac{1}{2}$ tsp. ground cinnamon or allspice
$\frac{1}{2}$ cup raisins
4 tbsp. pine nuts, lightly toasted
4 ripe plum tomatoes, deseeded and chopped
$\frac{1}{4}$ cup white wine

4 anchovy fillets, chopped
$\frac{1}{2}$ bunch chopped fresh parsley
$\frac{1}{2}$ bunch chopped fresh mint
6 tbsp. freshly grated Parmesan cheese
salt and pepper
fresh tomato sauce, to serve (optional)

1 Using a sharp knife, slice off the tops of the bell peppers, then remove the cores and seeds. Blanch the bell peppers in boiling water for 2–3 minutes. Carefully remove and drain upside down on a wire rack.

2 Bring a saucepan of salted water to a boil. Gradually pour in the rice and return to a boil; simmer until tender, but firm to the bite. Drain and rinse under cold running water. Set aside.

3 Heat the oil in a large skillet. Add the onion and celery and cook for 2 minutes. Stir in the garlic, cinnamon, and raisins and cook for 1 minute. Fork in the rice, then stir in the pine nuts, tomatoes, wine, anchovies, parsley, and mint and cook for 4 minutes. Remove from the heat, add salt and pepper, and stir in half the Parmesan.

4 Brush the bottom of a baking dish with a little oil. Divide the rice mixture equally among the peppers. Arrange in the dish and sprinkle with the remaining Parmesan. Drizzle with a little more oil and pour in enough water to come $\frac{1}{2}$ inch up the sides of the peppers. Loosely cover the dish with kitchen foil.

5 Bake in a preheated oven at 350°F for about 40 minutes. Uncover and cook for a further 10 minutes. Serve hot with tomato sauce.

Jamaican Rice and Peas

A favorite Caribbean dish, this was probably originally made with "pigeon peas," but you can use any dried bean you like. The spicy salsa is a modern twist to this all-in-one dish.

Serves 6–8

INGREDIENTS

2 cups dried beans, such as black-eyed beans, black beans, or small red kidney beans, soaked in cold water overnight

2 tbsp. vegetable oil

1 large onion, chopped

2–3 garlic cloves, finely chopped

2 red chilies, deseeded and chopped

2¼ cups long-grain white rice

⅔ cup canned coconut milk

¾ tsp. dried thyme

salt

TOMATO SALSA:

4 ripe tomatoes, deseeded and cut into ¼ inch cubes

1 red onion, finely chopped

4 tbsp. chopped fresh cilantro

2 garlic cloves, finely chopped

1–2 jalapeño chilies, or to taste, deseeded and thinly sliced

1–2 tbsp. extra-virgin olive oil

1 tbsp. fresh lime juice

1 tsp. light brown sugar

salt and pepper

1 Drain the soaked beans, rinse, and put in a large pan. Cover with cold water by about 2 inches and bring to a boil, over high heat, skimming off any foam.

2 Boil the beans for about 10 minutes (to remove any toxins), drain, and rinse again. Return to the pan, cover with cold water again, and bring to a boil over high heat.

3 Reduce the heat and keep at a moderate simmer, partially covered, for about 1¼–1½ hours for black-eyed beans, 1½–2 hours for black beans, or 50–60 minutes for kidney beans, until tender. Drain reserving the cooking liquid.

4 Heat the oil in another pan. Add the onion and cook for about 2 minutes until soft. Stir in the garlic and chilies and cook for a further minute. Add the rice and stir until well coated.

5 Stir in the coconut milk, thyme, and about 1 teaspoon salt. Add the cooked beans and 2 cups of the reserved bean cooking liquid to cover; add more bean liquid if necessary. Bring the mixture to a boil, then reduce the heat to low, cover tightly, and cook for 20–25 minutes.

6 Meanwhile, make the salsa: combine all the ingredients in a bowl and let stand, loosely covered, at room temperature.

7 Remove the rice from the heat and stand, covered, for 5 minutes, then fork into a serving bowl. Serve hot with the salsa.

Creole Jambalaya

A rich, rice-based stew, combining a fabulous mix of meat and seafood with exciting peppery flavorings, Jambalaya captures the true essence of Creole cooking.

Serves 6–8

INGREDIENTS

2 tbsp. vegetable oil

3 oz. piece good-quality smoked ham, cut into bite-sized pieces

1/2 cup andouille or pure smoked pork sausage, such as Polish kielbasa, cut into chunks

2 large onions, finely chopped

3–4 stalks celery, finely chopped

2 green bell peppers, cored, deseeded, and finely chopped

2 garlic cloves, finely chopped

8 oz. boned chicken breast or thighs, skinned and cut into pieces

4 ripe tomatoes, skinned and chopped

3/4 cup tomato sauce or strained tomatoes

2 cups fish stock

2 cups long-grain white rice

4 scallions, cut into 1-inch pieces

9 oz. peeled raw shrimp, tails on, if desired

9 oz. cooked white crab meat

12 oysters, shucked, with their liquor

SEASONING MIX:

2 dried bay leaves

1 tsp. salt

1 1/2–2 tsp. cayenne pepper, or to taste

1 1/2 tsp. dried oregano

1 tsp. ground white pepper, or to taste

1 tsp. black pepper, or to taste

1 To make the seasoning mix, mix the ingredients in a bowl.

2 Heat the oil in a flameproof casserole over medium heat. Add the smoked ham and the sausage and cook for about 8 minutes, stirring frequently, until golden. Using a slotted spoon, transfer to a large plate.

3 Add the onions, celery, and bell peppers to the casserole and cook for about 4 minutes until just softened. Stir in the garlic, then remove and set aside.

4 Add the chicken pieces to the casserole and cook for 3–4 minutes until beginning to color. Stir in the seasoning mix to coat.

5 Return the ham, sausage, and vegetables to the casserole and stir to combine. Add the chopped tomatoes and tomato sauce, then pour in the stock. Bring to a boil.

6 Stir in the rice and reduce the heat to a simmer. Cook for about 12 minutes. Uncover, stir in the scallions and shrimp and cook, covered, for 4 minutes.

7 Add the crab meat and oysters with their liquor and gently stir in. Cook until the rice is just tender, and the oysters slightly firm. Remove from the heat and let stand, covered, for about 3 minutes before serving.

Murgh Pullau

This delicately flavored dish is from North India. Traditionally the meat and rice are cooked together for ease of preparation, but here they are cooked separately to ensure perfect timing.

Serves 4–6

INGREDIENTS

1³⁄₄ cups basmati rice

4 tbsp. ghee or butter

1 cup slivered almonds

³⁄₄ cup unsalted, shelled pistachio nuts

4–6 boned chicken breasts, skinned and each cut into 4 pieces

2 onions, thinly sliced

2 garlic cloves, chopped finely

1-inch piece fresh ginger root, peeled and chopped

6 green cardamom pods, lightly crushed

4–6 whole cloves

2 bay leaves

1 tsp. ground coriander

¹⁄₂ tsp. cayenne pepper

1 cup natural yogurt

1 cup heavy cream

2–4 tbsp. chopped fresh cilantro or mint

8 oz. seedless green grapes, halved if large

1 Bring a saucepan of salted water to a boil. Gradually pour in the rice, return to a boil, then simmer until the rice is just tender. Drain and rinse under cold running water; set aside.

2 Heat the ghee in a deep skillet over medium-high heat. Add the almonds and pistachios and cook for 3 minutes, stirring, until light golden. Remove and reserve.

3 Add the chicken to the pan and cook for about 5 minutes, turning, until golden. Remove and reserve. Add the onions to the pan. Cook for about 10 minutes until golden. Stir in the garlic and spices and cook for 3 minutes.

4 Add 2–3 tablespoons of the yogurt and cook, stirring, until all the moisture evaporates. Continue adding the rest of the yogurt in the same way.

5 Return the chicken and nuts to the pan and stir to coat. Stir in ¹⁄₂ cup boiling water. Season with salt and pepper. Cook, covered, over low heat for about 10 minutes until the chicken is cooked through. Stir in the cream, cilantro, and grapes and remove from the heat.

6 Fork the rice into a bowl. Gently fold in the chicken and sauce. Let stand for 5 minutes. Serve.

Mumbar

This Middle Eastern dish is basically a long sausage coiled into a skillet to simmer.
The baharat, or spice mix, is typical of much of the cooking in the Gulf, as is basmati rice and onions.

Serves 6–8

INGREDIENTS

½ cup basmati rice
2 lb. ground lamb
1 small onion, finely chopped
3–4 garlic cloves, crushed
1 bunch each flat-leaf parsley and
   cilantro, finely chopped
2–3 tbsp. tomato ketchup

1 tbsp. vegetable oil
pared rind and juice of 1 lime
3 cups hot lamb stock
salt and pepper

BAHARAT SEASONING MIX:
2 tbsp. black peppercorns

1 tbsp. coriander seeds
2 tsp. whole cloves
1½ tsp. cumin seeds
1 tsp. cardamom seeds
1 cinnamon stick, broken into small pieces
1 whole nutmeg
2 tbsp. hot paprika

1 To make the baharat, grind the first 6 ingredients into a fine powder. Grate the whole nutmeg into the mix and stir in the paprika. Store in an airtight jar.

2 Bring a pan of salted water to a boil. Pour in the rice, return to a boil, then simmer until the rice is tender, but firm to the bite. Drain and rinse.

3 Place the lamb in a large bowl and break up with a fork. Add the onion, garlic, parsley, cilantro, ketchup, and 1 teaspoon of the baharat. Stir in the cooked rice and season. Squeeze the mixture to make it paste-like.

4 Divide into 4-6 pieces and roll each into a sausage of 1 inch thick. Brush a 9–10 inch skillet with the oil. Starting in the center of the pan, coil the sausage pieces, joining each piece, to form one long coiled sausage.

5 Press lightly to make an even layer, then tuck the lime rind between the spaces of the sausage. Add the lime juice to the pan. Pour in the hot stock and cover with a heatproof plate to keep in place.

6 Bring to a boil, then simmer gently for about 10 minutes. Cover; continue to cook for 15 minutes. Remove from the heat, drain, and slide the sausage onto a serving plate. Sprinkle with a little more of the baharat to serve.

Lamb Biriyani

For an authentic finishing touch, garnish with crisply-fried onion rings,
toasted slivered almonds, chopped pistachio nuts, and pieces of edible silver foil (vark).

Serves 6–8

INGREDIENTS

2 lb. boned lean leg or shoulder of
  lamb, cut into 1-inch cubes
6 garlic cloves, finely chopped
1¹⁄₂-inch piece fresh ginger root,
  peeled and finely chopped
1 tbsp. ground cinnamon
1 tbsp. green cardamom pods, crushed
  to expose the black seeds
1 tsp. whole cloves
2 tsp. coriander seeds, crushed
2 tsp. cumin seeds, crushed

¹⁄₂ tsp. ground turmeric (optional)
2 fresh green chilies, deseeded and
  chopped
grated rind and juice of 1 lime
1 bunch fresh cilantro, chopped finely
1 bunch fresh mint, chopped finely
¹⁄₂ cup natural yogurt
8 tbsp. ghee, butter, or vegetable oil
4 onions, 3 thinly sliced and 1 finely
  chopped
3 cups basmati rice

2 cinnamon sticks, broken
¹⁄₂ a whole nutmeg, freshly grated
3–4 tbsp. raisins
5 cups chicken stock or water
1 cup hot milk
1 tsp. saffron threads, slightly crushed
salt and pepper

1 Combine the lamb with the garlic, ginger, cinnamon, cardamom, cloves, coriander and cumin seeds, turmeric, chilies, lime rind and juice, 2 tablespoons each of coriander and mint, and yogurt. Marinate for 2–3 hours.

2 Heat about half the fat in a large skillet, add the sliced onions, and cook for about 8 minutes until lightly browned. Add the meat and any juices; season with salt and pepper. Stir in about 1 cup water and simmer for 18–20 minutes until the lamb is just cooked.

3 Meanwhile, heat the fat left over in a flameproof casserole. Add the chopped onion and cook for 2 minutes until soft. Add the rice and cook, stirring, for 3–4 minutes until well coated. Add the cinnamon, nutmeg, raisins, and stock. Bring to a boil, stirring once or twice, and season with salt and pepper. Simmer, covered, over low heat for 12 minutes until the liquid is reduced but the rice is still a little firm.

4 Pour the hot milk over the saffron; let stand for 10 minutes. Remove the rice from the heat and stir in the saffron-milk. Fold in the lamb mixture. Cover and bake in a preheated oven at 180°F until the rice is cooked and the liquid absorbed.

Red Pork Curry with Jasmine-scented Rice

Thai food has become so popular in recent years that most ingredients can be found in your local supermarket. Using a food processor may not be authentic, but it saves time and energy.

Serves 4–6

INGREDIENTS

2 lb. boned pork shoulder, cut into thin slices

3 cups coconut milk

2 fresh red chilies, deseeded and thinly sliced

2 tbsp. Thai fish sauce

2 tsp. brown sugar

1 large red bell pepper, cored, deseeded, and thinly sliced

6 kaffir lime leaves, shredded

½ bunch fresh mint leaves, shredded

½ bunch Thai basil leaves or Italian-style basil, shredded

jasmine-scented or Thai fragrant rice, cooked according to the package instructions and kept warm

RED CURRY PASTE:

1 tbsp. coriander seeds

2 tsp. cumin seeds

2 tsp. black or white peppercorns

1 tsp. salt, or to taste

5–8 dried hot red chilies

3–4 shallots, chopped

6–8 garlic cloves

2-inch piece fresh galangal or ginger root, peeled and coarsely chopped

2 tsp. kaffir lime rind or 2 fresh lime leaves, chopped

1 tbsp. ground red chili powder

1 tbsp. shrimp paste

2 stalks lemon grass, thinly sliced

1 To make the red curry paste, grind the coriander seeds, cumin seeds, peppercorns, and salt to a fine powder. Add the chilies, one by one, according to taste, until ground.

2 Put the shallots, garlic, galangal or ginger root, kaffir lime rind, chili powder, and

shrimp paste in a food processor. Process for about 1 minute. Add the ground spices and process again. Adding water, a few drops at a time, continue to process until a thick paste forms. Scrape into a bowl and stir in the lemon grass.

3 Put about half the red curry paste in a large, deep, heavy-

based skillet with the pork. Cook over medium heat for 2–3 minutes, stirring gently, until the pork is evenly coated and begins to brown.

4 Stir in the coconut milk and bring to a boil. Cook, stirring frequently, for about 10 minutes. Reduce the heat, stir in the chilies, Thai fish sauce, and brown sugar and simmer for about 20 minutes. Add the red bell pepper and simmer for a further 10 minutes.

5 Add the lime leaves and half the mint and basil to the curry. Transfer to a serving dish, sprinkle with the remaining mint and basil, and serve with the rice.

Mee Krob

Everyone loves the spiciness and crunch of this traditional Thai noodle dish.
Fry the rice noodles little by little to avoid too much spattering and smoke during cooking.

Serves 4–6

INGREDIENTS

vegetable oil, for frying

12 oz. fine rice vermicelli noodles, unsoaked

4 eggs, lightly beaten

3 oz. boned lean leg of pork, thinly sliced

3 oz. boned chicken breast, skinned and thinly sliced

3 oz. small peeled shrimp

4–6 scallions, thinly sliced on the diagonal

3–4 fresh red chilies, thinly sliced on the diagonal

4 tbsp. rice vinegar

4 tbsp. light soy sauce

4 tbsp. Thai fish sauce

4–6 tbsp. chicken stock or water

4 tbsp. sugar

1 tsp. coriander seeds, lightly crushed

4 tbsp. chopped fresh cilantro

1 Heat at least 3 inches of vegetable oil in a deep-fat fryer or wok to 350–375°F or until a cube of bread browns in 30 seconds.

2 Gently separate the layers of noodles, then carefully fry, one layer at a time, for 10–15 seconds until golden. Transfer to paper towels to drain; set aside.

3 Heat 1–2 tablespoons of the hot oil in a large non-stick skillet.

Pour in the beaten egg to form a thin layer and cook for about 1 minute until just set. Turn and cook for 5 seconds longer. Slide out of the pan and cool slightly. Cut in half and roll up each half, then slice into ¼-inch strips. Set aside.

4 Heat 2 more tablespoons of the oil in a wok or large, deep skillet over medium-high heat. Add the pork and chicken slices and stir-fry for about 2 minutes, or until cooked.

5 Add the shrimp, scallions, and chilies and stir to mix. Push the meat and vegetables to one side. Add the vinegar, soy sauce, fish sauce, sugar, and coriander seeds to the space in the pan, simmer gently, then stir into the meat mixture. Stir in the omelet and half the fresh cilantro.

6 Add the warm noodles, turn gently, and sprinkle with the remaining cilantro.

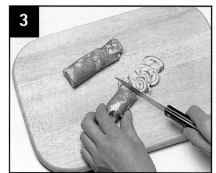

Nasi Goreng

A meal in itself, this mouthwatering fried rice dish is bursting with the exotic flavors of Indonesia. The perfect supper dish!

Serves 4

INGREDIENTS

1 large onion, chopped
2–3 garlic cloves
1 tsp. shrimp paste
2 red chilies, deseeded and chopped
vegetable oil
3 eggs, lightly beaten
1 lb. beef rump steak, about
　½ inch thick
2 carrots, cut into thin matchsticks

6 oz. Chinese long beans or green
　beans, cut into 1-inch pieces
6 small scallions, cut into ½-inch
　pieces
9 oz. raw shelled shrimp
3¾ cups cooked long-grain white rice,
　at room temperature
6 tbsp. dark soy sauce

TO GARNISH:
4 tbsp. ready-fried onion flakes
4 inch piece cucumber, deseeded and
　cut into thin sticks
2 tbsp. chopped fresh cilantro

1 Put the onion, garlic, shrimp paste, and chilies into a food processor and process until a paste forms. Add a little oil and process until smooth. Set aside.

2 Heat 1–2 tablespoons oil in a large, non-stick skillet. Pour in the egg to form a thin layer and cook for 1 minute until just set. Turn and cook for 5 seconds on the other side. Slide out and cut in half. Roll up each half, then slice into ¼-inch wide strips. Set aside.

3 Heat 2 tablespoons oil in the same pan over high heat and add the steak. Cook for 2 minutes on each side to brown and seal, but do not cook completely. Cool, then cut into thin strips and reserve.

4 Heat 2 tablespoons oil in a large wok over medium-high heat. Add the reserved chili paste and cook, stirring frequently, for about 3 minutes. Add 2 tablespoons of oil, the carrots, and long beans. Stir-fry for about 2 minutes. Add the scallions, shrimp, and the beef strips and stir-fry until the shrimp are pink.

5 Stir in the rice, half the sliced omelet, 2 tablespoons soy sauce, and ¼ cup water. Cover and steam for 1 minute. Spoon into a serving dish, top with the remaining omelet, and drizzle with the remaining soy sauce. Sprinkle with a selection of the garnishes and serve.

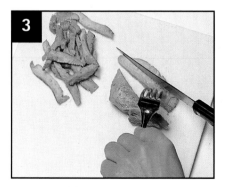

Iranian Steamed Crusty Rice

The trick is to achieve a light fragrant rice with a crunchy golden brown crust;
it may take several attempts, but it's worth the effort!

Serves 6

INGREDIENTS

2 cups plus 1 tbsp. basmati or long-grain white rice	salt 4 tbsp. butter or ghee	¼ cup water

1 Bring at least 8 cups of water to a boil. Add 2 tablespoons of salt. Gradually add the rice, then simmer for 7–10 minutes until almost tender; stir gently occasionally. Drain and rinse under warm running water to remove any starch.

2 Heat the butter or ghee with the water in a large heavy-based saucepan over medium-high heat until the butter melts and the water is steaming; remove half of this mixture and reserve. Spoon enough rice into the pan to cover the bottom, smoothing lightly and evenly.

3 Spoon the remaining rice into the pan. Cover the rice with a thin dish towel, then cover the pan tightly and reduce the heat to very low. Cook for 15 minutes.

4 Remove the covers and, with the handle of a wooden spoon, gently poke several holes into the rice to allow the steam to escape.

5 Pour the remaining butter-water mixture over the rice, re-cover as before, and cook for 10–15 minutes. Uncover and transfer the pan to a chilled surface (see Cook's Tip); this helps to loosen the crust from the bottom.

6 Using a fork, fluff the loose rice into a serving bowl. Break up the crusty brown layer into pieces and arrange around the serving dish. Traditionally, the honored guest got the crusty layer!

COOK'S TIP

To chill the work surface for cooling down the saucepan of hot rice, place 2 ice-cube trays on the work surface ahead of time.

Chinese Fried Rice

This simple Cantonese recipe for using leftover rice has become a world-wide specialty in Chinese restaurants. Enjoy this homemade version, which includes ham and shrimp.

Serves 4–6

INGREDIENTS

2–3 tbsp. peanut or vegetable oil

2 onions, halved and cut lengthwise into thin wedges

2 garlic cloves, thinly sliced

1-inch piece fresh ginger root, peeled, sliced, and cut into slivers

7 oz. cooked ham, thinly sliced

4 cups cooked, cold long-grain white rice

9 oz. cooked peeled shrimp

4 oz. canned water chestnuts, sliced

3 eggs

3 tsp. sesame oil

4–6 scallions, diagonally sliced into 1-inch pieces

2 tbsp. dark soy sauce or Thai fish sauce

1 tbsp. sweet chili sauce

2 tbsp. chopped fresh cilantro or flat-leaf parsley

salt and pepper

1 Heat 2–3 tablespoons peanut oil in a wok or large, deep skillet until very hot. Add the onions and stir-fry for about 2 minutes until beginning to soften. Add the garlic and ginger and stir-fry for another minute. Add the ham strips and stir to combine.

2 Add the cold cooked rice and stir to mix with the vegetables and ham. Stir in the shrimp and the water chestnuts.

Stir in 2 tablespoons water and cover the pan quickly. Continue to cook for 2 minutes, shaking the pan occasionally to prevent sticking and to allow the rice to heat through.

3 Beat the eggs with 1 teaspoon of the sesame oil and season with salt and pepper. Make a well in the center of the rice mixture, add the eggs, and immediately stir, gradually drawing the rice into the eggs.

4 Stir in the scallions, soy sauce, and chili sauce and stir-fry; stir in a little more water if the rice looks dry or is sticking. Drizzle in the remaining sesame oil and stir. Season to taste with salt and pepper.

5 Remove from the heat, wipe the edge of the wok or skillet, and sprinkle with the cilantro. Serve immediately from the pan.

Malayan Rice Noodle Soup

This meal-in-a-bowl soup is based on a dish called
Laska in Malayan and has a very authentic flavor.

Serves 4–6

INGREDIENTS

2 lb. 12 oz. corn-fed or
   free-range chicken
1 tsp. black peppercorns
2 tbsp. peanut or vegetable oil
2 onions, thinly sliced
2–3 garlic cloves, minced
1-inch piece fresh ginger root, peeled
   and thinly sliced
1 tsp. ground coriander

2 fresh red chilies, deseeded and thinly
   sliced on the diagonal
$\frac{1}{2}$–1 tsp. ground turmeric
1–2 tsp. Madras curry paste
$1\frac{2}{3}$ cups canned coconut milk
1 lb. large raw shrimp, peeled and
   deveined
$\frac{1}{2}$ small head of Chinese leaves, thinly
   shredded
1 tsp. sugar

2 scallions, thinly sliced
4 oz. bean sprouts
9 oz. rice noodles, rice vermicelli, or
   rice sticks, soaked according to
   package instructions
handful of fresh mint leaves, to garnish

1 To make the stock, put the chicken in a large saucepan with the peppercorns and enough cold water just to cover. Bring to a boil, then simmer for 1 hour, skimming off any foam.

2 Remove the chicken; cool. Skim any fat from the liquid and strain through muslin; set aside. Remove the chicken meat from the carcass and shred.

3 Heat the oil in a deep skillet until very hot. Add the onions to the pan and stir-fry for about 2 minutes until they begin to color. Stir in the garlic, ginger, coriander, chilies, turmeric, and curry paste. Transfer to a large pan and slowly stir in the stock. Simmer, partially covered, over low heat for about 20 minutes or until the stock has slightly reduced.

4 Add the coconut milk, shrimp, and Chinese leaves to the simmering stock; cook for about 3 minutes, stirring occasionally, until the shrimp are pink. Add the shredded chicken and cook for a further 2 minutes.

5 Drain the noodles and divide between 4–6 bowls. Ladle the hot stock and vegetables over the noodles. Make sure each serving has some of the shrimp and the shredded chicken. Garnish with mint leaves and serve immediately.

COOK'S TIP

Corn-fed chickens are reared on a diet of corn, which gives them a distinctive yellow color and delicious flavor.

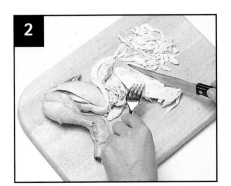

Singapore Noodles

*Although called Singapore noodles, this spicy rice noodle dish probably evolved in Hong Kong,
where the diverse cultures of Southeast Asia often come together.*

Serves 4–6

INGREDIENTS

2 oz. dried Chinese mushrooms

8 oz. rice vermicelli noodles

2–3 tbsp. peanut or vegetable oil

6–8 garlic cloves, thinly sliced

2–3 shallots, thinly sliced

1-inch piece fresh ginger root, peeled
and thinly sliced

4–5 fresh red chilies, deseeded and
thinly sliced on the diagonal

8 oz. boned chicken breasts, skinned
and thinly sliced

8 oz. snow peas, thinly sliced on the
diagonal

8 oz. Chinese leaves, thinly shredded

8 oz. cooked peeled shrimp

6–8 water chestnuts, sliced

2 scallions, thinly sliced on the
diagonal

2 tbsp. chopped fresh cilantro or mint

SINGAPORE CURRY SAUCE:

2 tbsp. rice wine or dry sherry

2 tbsp. soy sauce

3 tbsp. medium or hot Madras curry
powder

1 tbsp. sugar

$1^{2}/_{3}$ cups canned coconut milk

1 tsp. salt

fresh-ground black pepper to taste

1 To make the curry sauce, whisk the rice wine and soy sauce into the curry powder, then stir in the remaining ingredients.

2 Put the Chinese mushrooms in a small bowl and add enough boiling water to cover. Soak for about 15 minutes until softened. Lift out and squeeze out the liquid. Discard any stems, then slice thinly and set aside. Soak the rice noodles according to the instructions on the package, then drain well.

3 Heat the oil in a wok or deep skillet over medium-high heat. Add the garlic, shallots, ginger, and chilies and stir-fry for about 30 seconds. Add the chicken and snow peas and stir-fry for about 2 minutes. Add the Chinese leaves, shrimp, water chestnuts, mushrooms, and scallions and stir-fry for 1–2 minutes. Add the curry sauce and noodles; stir-fry for 5 minutes. Add the cilantro; serve.

Vietnamese Spring Rolls

Vietnamese spring rolls use a very thin rice paper as a wrapper which gives them their characteristic thin, crisp texture.

Makes 25–30 rolls

INGREDIENTS

25–30 rice paper wrappers
4–5 tbsp. all-purpose flour, mixed to a
    paste with 4–5 tbsp. water
vegetable oil, for frying
sliced scallions, to garnish

FILLING:
¹/₂ oz. dried Chinese mushrooms
1–2 tbsp. peanut or vegetable oil
1 small onion, finely chopped

3–4 garlic cloves
1¹/₂-inch piece fresh ginger root, peeled
    and chopped
8 oz. ground pork
2 scallions, finely chopped
4 oz. fresh bean sprouts
4 water chestnuts, chopped
2 tbsp. fresh chives, thinly sliced
6 oz. small cooked peeled shrimp,
    coarsely chopped

1 tsp. oyster sauce
1 tsp. light soy sauce
2 oz. rice vermicelli or cellophane
    noodles, soaked according to package
    instructions
salt and pepper

1 To make the filling, cover the Chinese mushrooms with boiling water. Let stand for about 15 minutes until softened. and squeeze out the liquid. Discard any stems and slice thinly.

2 Heat the oil in a wok over high heat. Add the onion, garlic, and ginger and stir-fry for 2 minutes. Add the pork and soaked mushrooms and stir-fry for about 4 minutes until the pork is cooked and any liquid evaporates. Stir in the scallions. Transfer to a bowl; cool.

3 Stir in the bean sprouts, water chestnuts, chives, and shrimp with the oyster and soy sauces. Season with salt and pepper. Add the noodles and toss.

4 To assemble the spring rolls, soften a rice paper wrapper in warm water for a few seconds, then drain on a clean dry dish towel. Put 2 tablespoons of the filling near one edge of the wrapper, fold the edge over the filling to cover, then fold in each side and roll up. Seal with a little of the flour paste; set aside. Make the remaining rolls.

5 Heat about 4 inches of oil in a deep-fat fryer to 350–375°F or until a cube of bread browns in 30 seconds. Fry the spring rolls a few at a time for about 2 minutes, turning once or twice, until golden. Drain on paper towels, then serve garnished with scallions.

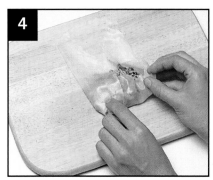

Japanese Sushi

These little snacks are made with special seasoned rice and a variety of toppings. Mix any remaining rice with the salmon trimmings and roll in toasted sesame seeds.

Serves 4–6

INGREDIENTS

2 cups sushi rice
4 tbsp. Japanese rice vinegar
1½ tbsp. superfine sugar
1½ tsp. salt
1½ tbsp. mirin (Japanese rice wine)

NORIMAKI SUSHI:
2 eggs
pinch of turmeric
1–2 tbsp. vegetable oil

4 sheets dried nori seaweed
4 oz. smoked salmon slices, cut into
    3-inch pieces
½ cucumber, lightly peeled, quartered,
    deseeded, then thinly sliced lengthwise
fresh chives

NIGIRI SUSHI:
16 cooked peeled shrimp
wasabi paste (Japanese horseradish)
3 oz. smoked salmon fillet, cut into
    ¼-inch slices
sesame seeds, lightly toasted

TO SERVE:
pickled ginger
Japanese soy sauce

1 Bring 2⅛ cups water and the rice to a boil, then simmer, covered, for 20 minutes until just tender. Let stand for 10 minutes, covered.

2 Bring to a boil the vinegar, sugar, salt, and mirin. Pour the vinegar mixture evenly over the surface of the rice. Quickly blend into the rice, fanning the rice at the same time as it cools.

3 For the norimaki sushi, beat the eggs with the turmeric and 1 teaspoon of the oil, then use to make 2 omelets, cooking in the remaining oil. Cut in half.

4 Pass the sheets of nori over a flame for a few minutes to toast. Lay a piece of nori, toasted-side down, on a bamboo sushi mat. Lay an omelet half on top, leaving a border around the edge.

Spread a thin layer of sushi rice over. Place a piece of smoked salmon on the bottom third of the rice, trimming to fit, and top with cucumber slices and a few chives.

5 Moisten the border of the nori with a little water and, using the mat as a guide, roll up. Repeat with the rest and allow to set, seam-side down. Cut into 1-inch slices, cover, and chill.

6 For the nigiri sushi, using wet hands, shape 2 tablespoons of the rice at a time into oblongs or ovals. Top with 2 shrimp, or a dab of wasabi and some smoked salmon. Sprinkle with the toasted sesame seeds. Serve the sushi with the pickled ginger and Japanese soy sauce.

Puddings, Cakes, & Pastries

One of the best ways to use rice is in desserts. Its delicate flavor and starchy characteristics are ideal for many puddings, cakes, and sweets. Who can resist Meringue-Topped Rice Pudding, a thick creamy vanilla-scented rice topped with a sweet golden meringue—the perfect dessert for a cold winter night?

Every nationality seems to have developed a rice pudding, from the grand molded Riz à l'Impératrice of France, to the classic Indian rice pudding, Kesari Kheer, which is tinted a stunning yellow with saffron. Sometimes only ground rice or rice flour is cooked with milk until it thickens into a rich creamy dish, as in the Lebanese Almond Rice Pudding—absolutely delicious.

Rice gives texture to cakes such as the Italian Lemon Rice Cake, a divine creation flavored with rum and dried fruit, and the Rice Muffins, delicious with amaretto butter. An Italian ice cream is given an interesting twist with the addition of rice, while Spicy Carrot-rice Cake is a variation on an old favorite. Rice flour replaces a little flour in baked goods such as Scottish Shortbread and Persian Rice Cookies, where it lends a fine texture and delicate flavor.

Meringue-topped Rice Pudding

*Probably Scandinavian in origin, this mouthwatering pudding is thickened with
cornstarch and egg yolks, making it extra rich and comforting.*

Serves 6–8

INGREDIENTS

½ cup water
5 cups milk
½ cup long-grain white rice
2–3 strips of lemon rind
1 cinnamon stick

1 vanilla bean, split
⅔ cup sugar
3 tbsp. cornstarch
4 egg yolks

MERINGUE:
6 egg whites
¼ tsp. cream of tartar
1 cup plus 2 tbsp. superfine sugar

1 Bring the water and 1 cup of the milk to a boil in a large heavy-based saucepan. Add the rice, lemon rind, cinnamon stick, and vanilla bean and reduce the heat to low. Cover and simmer for about 20 minutes until the rice is tender and all the liquid is absorbed. Remove the lemon rind, cinnamon stick, and vanilla bean and add the remaining milk; return to a boil.

2 Stir together the sugar and the cornstarch. Stir in a little of the hot rice-milk to make a paste, then stir into the pan of rice. Cook, stirring constantly, until the mixture boils and thickens. Boil for 1 minute, then remove from the heat to cool slightly.

3 Beat the egg yolks until smooth. Stir a large spoonful of the hot rice mixture into the yolks, beating until well blended, then stir into the rice mixture. Pour into a 12-cup baking dish.

4 To make the meringue, beat the egg whites with the cream of tartar in a large bowl to form stiff peaks. Add the sugar, 2 tablespoons at a time, beating well after each addition, until stiff and glossy.

5 Gently spoon the meringue over the top of the rice pudding, spreading evenly. Make swirls with the back of the spoon.

6 Bake in a preheated oven at 300°F for about 1 hour until the top is golden and set. Turn off the oven, open the door, and allow the pudding to cool in the oven. Serve warm, at room temperature, or cold.

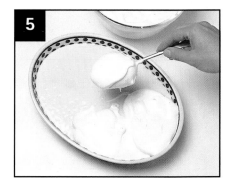

Basmati Pudding with Bay & Orange

This homely yet sophisticated rice pudding is surprisingly easy to make; the bay and orange are a delicious combination.

Serves 4

INGREDIENTS

2½ cups milk
1 cup light cream
4 fresh bay leaves, washed and gently
   bruised

4 tbsp. basmati or long-grain
   white rice
¼ cup sugar
2 tbsp. golden raisins or raisins
grated rind of 1 orange

1 tsp. vanilla extract
2 tbsp. pine nuts or green pistachios
fancy cookies, to serve

1 Put the milk and cream in a medium heavy-based saucepan and bring to a boil over medium heat, stirring occasionally to prevent sticking.

2 Add the bay leaves, then sprinkle in the rice. Reduce the heat to low and simmer gently for about 1 hour, stirring occasionally, until the rice is tender and the mixture is thickened and creamy.

3 Stir in the sugar, golden raisins, and orange rind and stir frequently until the sugar is dissolved and the fruit is plump. Remove from the heat, discard the bay leaves, and stir in the vanilla.

4 Meanwhile, toast the pine nuts in a small skillet until golden.

5 Spoon the pudding into individual bowls and sprinkle with the toasted nuts. Serve warm, or refrigerate to thicken and chill. Serve the biscuits separately.

VARIATION

Bay has a lovely flavor and goes well with rice, but, if preferred, you can substitute a cinnamon stick, lightly crushed cardamom seeds, freshly grated nutmeg, or seeds from a vanilla bean.

Raspberry Risotto with Glazed Raspberries

Why shouldn't risotto be served as a dessert? If you think about it,
most risottos are really savory rice puddings. This is really delicious—try it.

Serves 4–6

INGREDIENTS

2 cups milk

2 cups canned unsweetened coconut
  milk

pinch of salt

1 vanilla bean, split

2–3 strips lemon rind

2 tbsp. unsalted butter

²/₃ cup arborio rice

¹/₄ cup dry white vermouth

¹/₂ cup sugar

¹/₂ cup heavy or whipping cream

2–3 tbsp. raspberry-flavored liqueur

about 2 cups fresh raspberries

2 tbsp. good-quality raspberry jam or
  preserve

squeeze of lemon juice

toasted slivered almonds,
  to decorate (optional)

1 Heat the milk in a heavy-based saucepan with the coconut milk, salt, vanilla bean, and lemon rind until bubbles begin to form around the edge of the pan. Reduce the heat to low and keep the milk mixture hot, stirring occasionally.

2 Heat the butter in another large heavy-based pan over medium heat until foaming. Add the rice and cook, stirring, for 2 minutes to coat well.

3 Add the vermouth; it will bubble and steam rapidly. Cook, stirring, until the wine is completely absorbed. Gradually add the hot milk, about ½ cup at a time, allowing each addition to be absorbed completely before adding the next.

4 When half the milk has been added, stir in the sugar until dissolved. Continue stirring and adding the milk until the rice is tender, but still firm to the bite;

this should take about 25 minutes. Remove from the heat; remove the vanilla bean and lemon strips. Stir in half the cream, the liqueur, and half the fresh raspberries; cover.

5 Heat the raspberry jam with the lemon juice and 1–2 tablespoons water, stirring until smooth. Remove from heat, add the remaining raspberries and mix. Stir the remaining cream into the risotto and serve with the glazed raspberries. Decorate if desired.

Snowdon Pudding

This old-fashioned British steamed pudding was named after the Welsh mountain, Snowdon.
The story goes it was served to tired hungry climbers at the hotel at the foot of Mount Snowdon.

Serves 6

INGREDIENTS

butter, for greasing
³/₄ cup raisins
2 tbsp. chopped angelica
2 cups fresh white breadcrumbs
2 tbsp. rice flour
pinch of salt

1 cup plus 2 tbsp. shredded suet*
2 tbsp. light brown sugar
grated rind of 1 large lemon
2 eggs
¹/₃ cup marmalade
3–4 tsp. milk

LEMON SAUCE:
1 tbsp. cornstarch
1 cup plus 2 tbsp. milk
grated rind and juice of 2 lemons
3 tbsp. light corn syrup

* Ask your butcher for this

1 Sprinkle a well-buttered 5-cup pudding bowl with a tablespoon of the raisins and the angelica.

2 Put the remaining raisins in a bowl with the breadcrumbs, rice flour, salt, suet, sugar, and lemon rind and toss to combine. Make a well in the center.

3 Beat the eggs and marmalade for about 1 minute until beginning to lighten. Beat in 3 tablespoons of the milk; pour into the well. Gently stir into the dry ingredients to form a soft dough. Add more milk if necessary. Spoon into the prepared pudding bowl.

4 Butter a sheet of waxed paper and make a pleat along the center. Cover the basin loosely with the paper, buttered-side down; secure with string.

5 Stand the pudding bowl on a wire rack in a large pan. Fill with enough boiling water to come three quarters of the way up the side of the basin. Cover and steam gently over low heat for about 2 hours until the top is risen. Top up with boiling water when needed.

6 To make the lemon sauce, mix the cornstarch with about 3 tablespoons of milk to form a paste. Bring the remaining milk and the lemon rind to a simmer, then whisk into the paste until blended. Return the mixture to the pan and simmer gently for about 3 minutes, whisking, until smooth. Stir in the lemon juice and syrup. Pour into a pitcher; keep warm.

7 Remove the pudding from the pan, remove the paper, and allow the pudding to shrink slightly before unmolding. Serve hot with the lemon sauce.

Florentine Rice Pudding

*This very sophisticated rice pudding from Florence is like a cross between
a mousse and a souffle, and is best served warm.*

Serves 6

INGREDIENTS

¾ cup long-grain white rice or Italian
    arborio rice
pinch of salt
4 cups milk
5 eggs

2 cups sugar or 2 cups honey, or
    a mixture
8 tbsp. butter, melted and cooled
2 tbsp. orange flower water or
    4 tbsp. orange-flavored liqueur

8 oz. diced candied orange peel
about 1 cup orange marmalade
2–3 tablespoons water
confectioners' sugar, for dusting

1 Put the rice and salt in a large heavy-bottomed saucepan. Add the milk and bring to a boil, stirring occasionally. Reduce the heat to low and simmer gently for about 25 minutes until the rice is tender and creamy. Remove from heat.

2 Pass the cooked rice through a food mill into a large bowl. Alternatively, process in a food processor for about 30 seconds until smooth. Set aside. Stir from time to time to prevent a skin from forming.

3 Meanwhile, using an electric mixer, beat the eggs with the sugar in a large bowl for about 4 minutes until very light and creamy. Gently fold into the rice with the melted butter. Stir in half the orange flower water, then stir in the candied orange peel.

4 Pour into a well-buttered 8-cup souffle dish or charlotte mold. Place the dish in a roasting pan and pour in enough boiling water to come 1½ inches up the side of the dish.

5 Bake in a preheated oven at 350°F for about 25 minutes until puffed and lightly set. Transfer the dish to a wire rack to cool slightly.

6 Heat the marmalade with the water, stirring until dissolved and smooth. Stir in the remaining orange flower water and pour into a sauceboat or pitcher. Dust the top of the pudding with the confectioners' sugar and serve warm with the marmalade sauce.

Almond Rice Custard

This traditional Turkish sweet is simply an almond milk thickened with ground rice.
Serve with the traditional decoration of pistachios and pomegranate seeds if they are in season.

Serves 6

INGREDIENTS

³/₄ cup whole blanched almonds
4 cups milk
scant ¹/₄ cup rice flour
pinch of salt

¹/₄ cup sugar
¹/₂ tsp. almond extract or
  1 tbsp. almond-flavored liqueur
toasted slivered almonds, to decorate

TO SERVE (OPTIONAL):
12 oz. fresh strawberries, sliced,
  sprinkled with 2 tbsp. sugar and
  chilled

1 Put the almonds in a food processor and process until a thick paste forms. Bring 1 cup of the milk to a boil. Gradually pour into the almond paste, with the machine running, until the mixture is smooth. Let stand for about 10 minutes.

2 Combine the rice flour, salt, and sugar in a large bowl, then stir in about 4–5 tablespoons of the milk to form a smooth paste.

3 Bring the remaining milk to a boil in a heavy-based saucepan.

Pour the hot milk into the rice flour paste and stir constantly, then return the mixture to the saucepan and bring to a boil. Reduce the heat and simmer for about 10 minutes until smooth and thickened. Remove from the heat.

4 Strain the almond milk through a very fine strainer into the simmering rice custard, pressing the almonds through with the back of a spoon. Return to the heat and simmer for a further 7–10 minutes or until it becomes thick.

5 Remove from the heat and stir in the almond extract. Cool slightly, stirring, then pour into individual bowls. Sprinkle with the almonds and serve with the strawberries, if desired. Chill to serve later, if preferred—the custard will thicken as it cools.

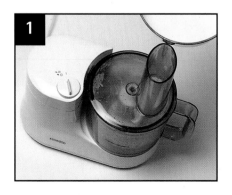

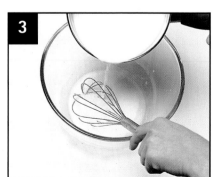

Black Rice Pudding with Mango Salad

This sticky black rice is like congee, the traditional rice porridge eaten all over Southeast Asia for breakfast or as a base for other dishes. Delicious with a mango salad.

Serves 6–8

INGREDIENTS

1½ cups black glutinous rice

3¾ cups boiling water

1 vanilla bean, split, black seeds removed and reserved

1 cup light brown sugar

2 oz. package coconut powder

14 fl. oz. can thick coconut milk

2 ripe mangoes

6 passion fruit

TO DECORATE:

shredded fresh coconut (optional)

fresh mint leaves, to decorate

1 Put the rice in a large heavy-based saucepan and pour the boiling water over. Add the vanilla bean and seeds to the pan. Return to a boil, stirring once or twice. Reduce the heat to low and simmer, covered, for about 25 minutes until the rice is tender and the liquid almost absorbed; do not uncover during cooking.

2 Remove from the heat and stir in the sugar, coconut powder, and half the coconut milk. Stir until the sugar is dissolved.

Cover and let stand for 10 minutes. If the rice becomes too thick, add a little more of the coconut milk or a little milk or water.

3 Cut each mango lengthwise along each side of the large stone to remove the flesh. Peel the mangoes, thinly slice, and arrange on a serving plate.

4 Cut the passion fruit crosswise in half and scoop out the pulp and juice; spoon

over the mango slices. Decorate with shredded coconut, if desired, and a few mint leaves.

5 Spoon the warm pudding into wide shallow bowls and decorate with shredded coconut and mint leaves. Drizzle some of the remaining coconut milk around the edges, if desired. Serve with the mango salad.

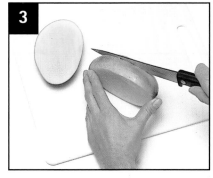

Rice Pudding Tartlets

These delicious little tartlets have a soft dark chocolate layer, covered with creamy rice pudding—
they make a scrumptious special occasion dessert or tea-time treat.

Makes 6–8 tartlets

INGREDIENTS

1 quantity Shortcrust Pastry (see page 150)
4 cups milk
pinch of salt
1 vanilla bean, split, seeds removed and reserved

1/2 cup arborio or long-grain white rice
1 tbsp. cornstarch
2 tbsp. sugar
cocoa powder, to dust
melted chocolate, to decorate

CHOCOLATE GANACHE:
3/4 cup heavy cream
1 tbsp. light corn syrup
6 oz. bitter-sweet or semi-sweet chocolate, chopped
1 tbsp. unsalted butter

1 Make the pastry shells following Steps 1–4 on page 150, increasing the sugar to 2 tablespoons. After removing the beans in Step 4, bake for 5–7 minutes longer until the pastry shells are crisp. Transfer the tartlets to a wire rack to cool.

2 To make the chocolate ganache, bring the heavy cream and corn syrup to a boil. Remove from the heat and immediately stir in the chopped chocolate; stir until melted and smooth. Beat in the butter. Spoon a 1-inch thick layer into each tartlet. Set aside.

3 Bring the milk and salt to a boil in a saucepan. Sprinkle in the rice and return to a boil. Add the vanilla seeds and pod. Reduce the heat and simmer until the rice is tender and the milk creamy.

4 Blend the cornstarch and sugar in a small bowl and add about 2 tablespoons water to make a paste. Stir in a few spoonfuls of the rice mixture, then stir the cornstarch mixture into the rice. Bring to a boil and cook for about 1 minute until thickened. Cool the pan in iced water, stirring until thick.

5 Spoon into the tartlets, filling each to the brim. Leave to set at room temperature. To serve, dust with cocoa powder and pipe or drizzle with melted chocolate.

Riz à l'Impératrice

This rich molded rice pudding is a classic French dessert. Serve with a sauce made by poaching dried apricots in water with apricot jam and lemon juice to taste, then processing until smooth.

Serves 6–8

INGREDIENTS

¹/₂ cup kirsch or other favorite liqueur
4 oz. candied or dried fruits, such as
   dried sour cherries, dried cranberries
   or blueberries, raisins, or candied peel
¹/₂ cup long-grain white rice
pinch of salt
3 cups milk

¹/₄ cup superfine sugar
1 vanilla bean, split open, seeds scraped
   out and reserved
1 envelope unflavored powdered gelatin
¹/₄ cup cold water
2 egg yolks, lightly beaten
1 cup heavy cream, whipped until soft
   peaks form

4 tbsp. apricot jam or preserve
glacé cherries, to decorate

1 Combine 2–3 tablespoons of the kirsch with the candied or dried fruits and set aside.

2 Bring a saucepan of water to a boil. Sprinkle in the rice and add the salt; simmer gently for 15–20 minutes until the rice is just tender. Drain, rinse, and drain again.

3 Bring the milk and sugar to a boil in a large non-stick saucepan. Add the vanilla seeds and bean and stir in the rice. Reduce the heat to low and simmer, covered, until the rice is very tender and the milk reduced by about a third. Remove from the heat and discard the vanilla bean.

4 Soften the gelatin in the water, then heat gently to dissolve.

5 Add about 2 tablespoons of the hot rice to the egg yolks and whisk to blend, then beat into the rice with the dissolved gelatin. until the mixture thickens slightly. Pour into a large mixing bowl. Place the bowl in a roasting pan half-filled with iced water and stir until beginning to set.

6 Fold in the soaked fruits and cream. Stir until it begins to set again, then immediately pour into a rinsed 5–6¹/₄ cup mold. Smooth the surface, cover, and chill for at least 2 hours or overnight.

7 Unmold the rice onto a serving plate. Heat the jam with the remaining kirsch and 2 tablespoons water to make a smooth glaze. Brush over the top of the unmolded rice. Decorate the dessert with cherries and let stand for 15 minutes before serving.

Chocolate Rice Dessert

What could be more delicious than creamy tender rice cooked in a rich chocolate sauce?
This dessert is almost like a dense chocolate mousse.

Serves 8–10

INGREDIENTS

¹/₂ cup long-grain white rice
pinch of salt
2 ¹/₂ cups milk
¹/₂ cup sugar

7 oz. bitter-sweet or semi-sweet
   chocolate, chopped
4 tbsp. butter, diced
1 tsp. vanilla extract
2 tbsp. brandy or Cognac

³/₄ cup heavy cream
whipped cream, for piping (optional)
chocolate curls, to decorate (optional)

1 Bring a saucepan of water to a boil. Sprinkle in the rice and add the salt; reduce the heat and simmer gently for 15–20 minutes until the rice is just tender. Drain, rinse, and drain again.

2 Heat the milk and the sugar in a large heavy-based saucepan over medium heat until the sugar dissolves, stirring frequently. Add the chocolate and butter and stir until melted and smooth.

3 Stir in the cooked rice and reduce the heat to low. Cover and simmer, stirring occasionally, for 30 minutes until the milk is absorbed and the mixture thickened. Stir in the vanilla extract and brandy. Remove from the heat and allow to cool to room temperature.

4 Using an electric mixer, beat the cream until soft peaks form. Stir one heaped spoonful of the cream into the chocolate rice mixture to lighten it; then fold in the remaining cream.

5 Spoon into glass serving dishes, cover, and chill for about 2 hours. If desired, decorate with piped whipped cream and top with chocolate curls. Serve cold.

VARIATION

To mold the chocolate rice, soften 1 envelope gelatin in about ¹/₄ cup cold water and heat gently until dissolved. Stir into the chocolate just before folding in the cream. Pour into a rinsed mold, allow to set, then unmold.

Orange-scented Rice Pudding

This delicious creamy pudding is flavored with fresh oranges,
orange-flavored liqueur, and two kinds of ginger for a wonderfully scented result.

Serves 6

INGREDIENTS

³/₄ cup pudding rice
1 cup freshly squeezed orange juice
pinch of salt
2¹/₄ cups milk
1 vanilla bean, split

2-inch piece fresh ginger root, peeled
  and gently bruised
1 cup sugar
¹/₄ cup heavy cream
4 tbsp. orange-flavored liqueur
2 tbsp. butter

4–6 seedless oranges
2 pieces stem ginger, sliced thinly, plus
  2 tbsp. ginger syrup from the jar
ground ginger, for dusting

1 Put the rice in a large heavy-based saucepan with the orange juice and salt. Bring to a boil, skimming off any foam. Reduce the heat to low and simmer gently for about 10 minutes, stirring occasionally, until the juice is absorbed.

2 Gradually stir in the milk, add the vanilla bean and ginger root, and continue to simmer for about 30 minutes, stirring frequently, until the milk is absorbed and the rice is very tender.

Remove from the heat; remove the vanilla bean and ginger root.

3 Stir in half the sugar, half the cream, the orange liqueur, and the butter until the sugar is dissolved and the butter is melted. Allow to cool, stir in the remaining cream and pour into a serving bowl. Let stand, covered, at room temperature.

4 Pare the rind from the oranges and reserve. Working over a bowl to catch the juices, remove the pith from all the

oranges. Cut out the segments and drop into the bowl. Stir in the stem ginger and syrup. Chill.

5 Cut the pared orange rind into thin strips and blanch for 1 minute. Drain and rinse. Bring 1 cup of water to a boil with the remaining sugar. Add the rind strips and simmer gently until the syrup is reduced by half. Cool.

6 Serve the pudding with the chilled oranges and top with the caramelized orange rind strips.

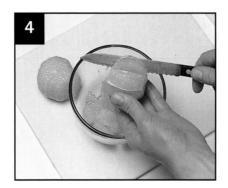

Kesari Kheer

This is a classic Indian milk pudding, full of exotic spices. This version contains saffron, which gives it a lovely deep-yellow color. The cream is not authentic, but does lighten the texture.

Serves 4–6

INGREDIENTS

2 tbsp. clarified butter or ghee
1/3 cup basmati rice, washed and well drained
6 1/4 cups milk
1/2 cup sugar or to taste

10–12 green cardamom pods, crushed to remove the black seeds (pods discarded)
1/2 cup golden raisins or raisins
large pinch saffron threads, about 1/2 tsp, soaked in 2–3 tbsp. milk
1/2 cup green pistachios, lightly toasted

2/3 cup heavy cream, whipped (optional)
ground cinnamon, for dusting
edible silver foil (vark), to decorate (optional)

1 Melt the butter in a large, heavy-based saucepan over medium heat. Pour in the rice and cook, stirring almost constantly, for about 6 minutes, until the rice grains are translucent and a deep golden brown.

2 Pour in the milk and over high heat bring to a boil. Reduce the heat to medium-high and simmer for about 30 minutes, stirring occasionally, until the milk has reduced by about half.

3 Add the sugar, cardamom seeds, and golden raisins and cook for about 20 minutes until reduced and thick. Stir in the saffron-milk mixture and simmer over low heat until as thick as possible, stirring almost constantly. Remove from the heat and stir in half the pistachios.

4 Place the saucepan in a larger pan of iced water and stir until cool. If using, stir in the cream, then spoon into a serving bowl and chill.

5 To serve, dust the top of the pudding with ground cinnamon. Sprinkle with the remaining pistachios and, if using, decorate with pieces of the silver foil (vark).

COOK'S TIP

The edible silver foil (vark) is available in some Asian or Indian supermarkets or specialty stores.

Lebanese Almond Rice Pudding

This delicate rice cream pudding is flavored with almonds and rosewater.
If pomegranates are in season, decorate with the gorgeous pink seeds for a stunning effect.

Serves 6

INGREDIENTS

¼ cup rice flour
pinch of salt
3 cups milk

¼ cup superfine sugar
¾ cup ground almonds
1 tbsp. rosewater

TO DECORATE:
2 tbsp. chopped pistachios or toasted
    slivered almonds
pomegranate seeds (optional)
washed rose petals (optional)

1 Put the rice flour in a bowl, stir in the salt, and make a well in the center.

2 Pour about ¼ cup of the milk into the well and whisk to form a smooth paste.

3 Bring the remaining milk to a boil in a heavy-based saucepan. Whisk in the rice flour paste and the sugar and cook, stirring continuously, until the mixture thickens and bubbles. Reduce the heat and simmer gently for 5 minutes.

4 Whisk in the ground almonds until the pudding is smooth and thickened, then remove from the heat to cool slightly. Stir in the rosewater and cool completely, stirring occasionally.

5 Divide the mixture between 6 glasses or pour into a serving bowl. Chill for at least 2 hours before serving.

6 To serve, sprinkle with the pistachios or almonds and pomegranate seeds, if available. Scatter with rose petals, if desired.

COOK'S TIP

For a smoother texture, this can be made without the ground almonds. Stir 2 tablespoons of cornstarch into the ground rice and use a little more of the milk to make the paste. Proceed as directed, omitting the ground almonds.

Portuguese Rice Pudding

*This buttery, egg-rich rice pudding
is quite irresistible!*

Serves 6–8

INGREDIENTS

1 cup Spanish valencia, Italian arborio,
   or pudding rice
pinch salt
1 lemon
2 cups milk

²/₃ cup light cream
1 cinnamon stick
6 tbsp. butter

³/₄ cup sugar (or to taste)
8 egg yolks
ground cinnamon, for dusting
thick or heavy cream, to serve

1 Bring a saucepan of water to a boil. Sprinkle in the rice and salt and return to a boil; reduce the heat and simmer until just tender. Drain, rinse, and drain.

2 Using a small sharp knife or swivel-bladed vegetable peeler, and working in a circular motion, try to peel the rind off the lemon in one curly piece; this makes it easier to remove later. Alternatively, peel off in strips.

3 Bring the milk and cream to a simmer over medium heat.

Add the rice, cinnamon stick, butter, and the lemon rind "curl" or strips. Reduce the heat to low and simmer gently for about 20 minutes until thick and creamy. Remove from the heat; remove and discard the cinnamon stick and the lemon rind. Stir in the sugar until dissolved.

4 In a large bowl, beat the egg yolks until well blended. Gradually beat in the rice mixture until thick and smooth. Continue to stir frequently to prevent the eggs from curdling, until slightly

cooled, then pour into a bowl or 6–8 individual glasses. Dust with ground cinnamon and serve at room temperature.

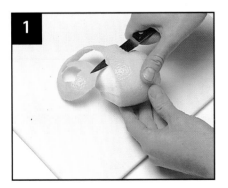

Rice Pudding Brulée

A thick creamy rice pudding with a crunchy, caramelized sugar topping. Do not refrigerate after caramelizing the puddings, as the condensation will make the sugar wet and soggy.

Serves 6–8

INGREDIENTS

1 cup arborio rice
pinch of salt
1 vanilla bean, split
scant 3 cups milk

1 cup superfine sugar
2 egg yolks
½ cup heavy or whipping cream
grated rind of 1 large lemon
4 tbsp. butter

2 tbsp. brandy or Cognac
light brown sugar, for glazing

1 Put the rice in a large heavy-based saucepan with a pinch of salt and add enough cold water to just cover. Bring to a boil, then reduce the heat and simmer gently for about 12 minutes until the water is absorbed.

2 Scrape the seeds from the split vanilla bean into the milk. Bring to a simmer and pour over the rice. Add the sugar, and cook over low heat, stirring, until the rice is tender and the milk thickened.

3 In a small bowl, beat the egg yolks with the cream and lemon rind. Stir in a large spoonful of the rice mixture and beat well to blend. Return the mixture to the pan and cook very gently until the pudding is thick and creamy; do not allow to boil. Stir in the butter.

4 Remove from the heat and stir in the brandy; remove the vanilla bean. Carefully spoon the mixture into 6–8 flameproof ramekins or crème brulée pots. Allow to cool, then chill for at least 2 hours.

5 Sprinkle a very thin layer of brown sugar on top of each ramekin, to cover completely. Wipe the edge of each ramekin, as the sugar may stick and burn.

6 Place the ramekins in a small roasting pan filled with about ½ inch iced water. Place under a preheated broiler, close to the heat, and broil until the sugar melts and caramelizes. Alternatively, use a small kitchen blowtorch to caramelize the sugar.

7 Cool the ramekins for 2–3 minutes before serving.

Italian Rice Ice Cream

*It stands to reason that a nation that thinks of risotto as its national dish should produce
a rice ice cream. Using a purchased lemon curd adds extra creaminess to the chewy rice texture.*

Makes about 1.2 litres/2 pints/5 cups

INGREDIENTS

$^1/_2$ cup short-grain pudding rice
2 $^1/_4$ cups milk
$^1/_3$ cup sugar
$^1/_3$ cup good-quality honey
$^1/_2$ tsp. lemon extract

1 tsp. vanilla extract
$^3/_4$ cup good-quality lemon curd
2$^1/_4$ cups heavy or whipping cream
grated rind and juice of 1 large lemon

1 Put the rice and milk in a large heavy-based saucepan and bring to a gentle simmer, stirring occasionally; do not allow to boil. Reduce the heat to low, cover, and simmer very gently for about 10 minutes, stirring occasionally, until the rice is just tender and the liquid absorbed.

2 Remove from the heat and stir in the sugar, honey, and vanilla and lemon extracts, stirring until the sugar is dissolved. Pour into a food processor and pulse 3 or 4 times. The mixture should be thick and creamy but not completely smooth.

3 Put the lemon curd in a bowl and gradually beat in about 1 cup of the cream. Stir in the rice mixture with the lemon rind and juice until blended. Lightly whip the remaining cream until it just begins to hold its shape, then fold into the lemon-rice mixture. Chill.

4 Stir the rice mixture and pour into an ice-cream machine. Churn according to the manufacturers' instructions for 15–20 minutes. Transfer to a freezerproof container and freeze for 6–8 hours or overnight. Transfer to the refrigerator about 1 hour before serving.

COOK'S TIP

If you do not have an ice-cream machine, transfer the chilled rice mixture to a freezerproof container. Freeze for 1 hour until slightly slushy, then whisk to break up any crystals; refreeze. Repeat twice more.

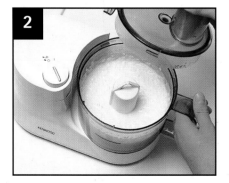

Scottish Shortbread

Many recipes for shortbread contain rice flour; combined with all-purpose flour it produces a delicate crisp shortbread cookie.

Makes 16 wedges

INGREDIENTS

2 cups all-purpose flour
½ cup rice flour
¼ tsp. salt

¾ cup unsalted butter, at room temperature
¼ cup superfine sugar

¼ cup confectioners' sugar, sifted
¼ tsp. vanilla extract (optional)
sugar, for sprinkling

1 Lightly grease two 8–9 inch cake or tart pans with removable bases. Sift the all-purpose flour, rice flour, and salt into a bowl; set aside.

2 Using an electric mixer, beat the butter for about 1 minute in a large bowl until creamy. Add the sugars and continue beating for 1–2 minutes until very light and fluffy. If using, beat in the vanilla.

3 Using a wooden spoon, stir the flour mixture into the butter and sugar until well blended. Turn onto a lightly floured surface and knead lightly to blend completely.

4 Divide the dough evenly between the 2 pans, smoothing the surface. Using a fork, press ¾-inch radiating lines around the edge of the dough. Lightly sprinkle the surfaces with a little sugar, then prick the surface lightly with the fork.

5 Using a sharp knife, mark each dough round into 8 wedges. Bake in a preheated oven at 250°F for 50–60 minutes until pale golden and crisp. Cool in the pans on a wire rack for about 5 minutes.

6 Carefully remove the side of each pan and slide the bottoms onto a heatproof surface. Using the knife marks as a guide, cut each shortbread into 8 wedges while still warm. Cool completely on the wire rack, then store in airtight containers.

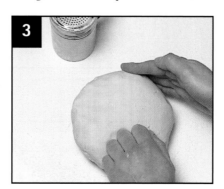

Persian Rice Crescents

These delicious little cookies made with rice flour have a fine texture and delicate flavor.
They are excellent with strong black coffee, or as an accompaniment to ice cream.

Makes about 60 crescents

INGREDIENTS

1 cup unsalted butter, softened
1 cup confectioners' sugar, sifted
2 egg yolks

$\frac{1}{2}$–1 tsp. ground cardamom or
  1 tbsp. rosewater
1$\frac{1}{2}$ cups rice flour, sifted
1 egg white, lightly beaten

$\frac{1}{2}$ cup finely chopped pistachio nuts
  or almonds

1 Using an electric mixer, beat the butter until light and creamy in a large bowl for about 1 minute. On low speed, gradually add the confectioners' sugar and beat for about 2 minutes until light and fluffy. Gradually add the egg yolks, beating well after each addition; then beat in the cardamom.

2 Gently stir the rice flour into the butter mixture to form a smooth, soft dough. Turn onto a lightly floured surface and knead lightly several times. Turn the mixing bowl over the dough and let rest about 1 hour.

3 Form heaped teaspoonfuls of the dough into balls, then form into crescent shapes. Place 2 inches apart on greased cookie sheets. Mark a pattern on the tops with a spoon.

4 Brush each cookie with a little beaten egg white and sprinkle with the chopped nuts.

5 Bake in a preheated oven at 350°C for about 15 minutes until the bases begin to color; the tops should remain very pale. Reduce the heat if the tops begin to color.

6 Cool on the cookie sheets for about 2 minutes, then transfer the cookies to wire racks to cool completely. Dust with confectioners' sugar and store in an airtight container.

COOK'S TIP

The new cooking-oil sprays are ideal for lightly greasing cookie sheets when making cookies.

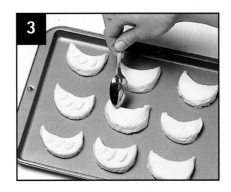

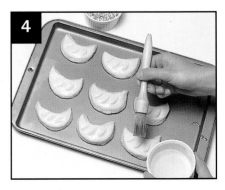

Chocolate Peanut Cookies

These delicious cookies contain two popular ingredients, peanuts and chocolate;
the rice flour gives them an original twist.

Makes 50–60 cookies

INGREDIENTS

1½ cups all-purpose flour
1½ cups rice flour
¼ cup unsweetened cocoa powder

1 tsp. baking powder
pinch salt
¾ cup vegetable shortening
1 cup superfine sugar

1 tsp. vanilla extract
1 cup raisins, chopped
1 cup unsalted peanuts, finely
  chopped
6 oz. bitter-sweet or semi-sweet
  chocolate, melted

1 Sift the flours, cocoa, baking powder, and salt into a bowl, then stir to combine.

2 Using an electric mixer, beat the fat and sugar in a large bowl for about 2 minutes until very light and creamy. Beat in the vanilla. Gradually blend in the flour mixture to form a soft dough. Stir in the raisins.

3 Put the chopped peanuts in a small bowl. Pinch off walnut-size pieces of the dough and roll into balls. Drop into the peanuts and roll to coat, pressing them lightly to stick. Place the balls about 3 inches apart on 2 large, greased, non-stick cookie sheets.

4 Using the flat bottom of a drinking glass dipped in flour, gently flatten each ball into a circle about ¼ inch thick.

5 Bake in a preheated oven at 350°F for about 10 minutes until golden and lightly set; do not overbake. Cool on the sheets for about 1 minute; then, using a thin palette knife, transfer to a wire rack to cool. Continue with the remaining dough and peanuts.

6 Arrange the cooled cookies close together on the wire rack and drizzle the tops with the melted chocolate. Allow to set before transferring to an airtight container with waxed paper between the layers.

Christmas Rice Pancakes

These delicious pancakes are almost like little rice puddings scented with Christmas mincemeat.
They make an elegant dessert, served with a custard flavored with raisins and rum.

Makes about 24 pancakes

INGREDIENTS

scant 3 cups milk
salt
$^1/_2$ cup long-grain white rice
1 cinnamon stick
$^1/_4$ cup sugar
$^1/_3$ cup all-purpose flour
1 tsp. baking powder

$^3/_4$ tsp. baking soda
2 eggs, beaten
$^1/_2$ cup sour cream
2 tbsp. dark rum
1 tsp. vanilla extract
$^1/_2$ tsp. almond extract
2 tbsp. butter, melted

12 oz. homemade or purchased
  mincemeat
melted butter, for frying
ground cinnamon, for dusting

1 To make the pancakes, bring the milk to a boil in a saucepan. Add a pinch of salt and sprinkle in the rice. Add the cinnamon stick and simmer gently for about 35 minutes, until the rice is tender and the milk almost absorbed.

2 Remove from the heat, add the sugar, and stir until dissolved. Discard the cinnamon stick and pour into a large bowl. Cool, stirring occasionally, for about 30 minutes.

3 Combine the flour, baking powder, baking soda, and a pinch of salt; set aside. Beat the eggs with the sour cream, rum, vanilla, and almond extracts, and the melted butter. Whisk the egg mixture into the rice, then stir in the flour mixture until just blended; do not over mix. Fold in the mincemeat.

4 Heat a large skillet or griddle, and brush with butter. Stir the batter and drop 2–3 tablespoons on to the pan. Cook for about 2 minutes until the undersides are

golden and the tops covered with bubbles that burst open. Gently turn, cook for another minute. Keep warm.

5 Dust the pancakes with cinnamon and serve.

COOK'S TIP

For a Christmas custard, soak 1cup raisins in boiling water. Bring 1½ cups milk to a boil. Scrape the seeds out of a vanilla bean and add to the milk with the bean. Bring back to a boil, remove from the heat, cover, and let stand for 10 minutes. Beat 5 eggs with sugar to taste until thick; beat in half the milk, then return the mixture to the pan. Cook until thickened; do not boil. Strain the raisins; add to the custard with 2–3 tbsp. dark rum. Serve chilled.

Rice Muffins with Amaretto Butter

Italian rice gives these delicate muffins an interesting texture. The amaretto cookies complement the flavors and add a wonderful crunchy topping.

Makes 12 muffins

INGREDIENTS

1¼ cups all-purpose flour
1 tbsp. baking powder
½ tsp. baking soda
½ tsp. salt
1 egg
¼ cup honey
½ cup milk

2 tbsp. sunflower oil
½ tsp. almond extract
1 cup cooked arborio rice
2–3 amaretto cookies, coarsely
  crushed

AMARETTO BUTTER:
8 tbsp. unsalted butter, at room
  temperature
1 tbsp. honey
1–2 tbsp. Amaretto liqueur
1–2 tbsp. mascarpone

1 Sift the flour, baking powder, baking soda, and salt into a large bowl and stir. Make a well in the center.

2 In another bowl, beat the egg, honey, milk, oil, and almond extract with an electric mixer for about 2 minutes until light and foamy. Gradually beat in the rice. Pour into the well and, using a fork, stir lightly until just combined. Do not over beat; the mixture can be slightly lumpy.

3 Spoon the batter into a lightly greased 12-cup muffin pan or two 6-cup pans. Sprinkle each with some of the amaretto cookie crumbs and bake in a preheated oven at 400°F for about 15 minutes until risen and golden; the tops should spring back lightly when pressed.

4 Cool in the pans on a wire rack for about 1 minute. Carefully remove the muffins and cool slightly.

5 To make the Amaretto butter, put the butter and honey in a small bowl and beat until creamy. Add the Amaretto and mascarpone and beat together. Spoon into a small serving bowl and serve with the warm muffins.

COOK'S TIP

Use paper liners to line the muffin pan cups to avoid sticking.

Mini Orange Rice Cakes

These mini rice cakes, fragrant with orange or sometimes lemon rind, are found in many of the bakeries and coffee shops in Florence. They are delicious with tea or coffee.

Makes about 16

INGREDIENTS

3 cups milk
pinch of salt
1 vanilla bean, split, seeds removed
   and reserved
1/2 cup arborio rice

1/2 cup sugar
2 tbsp. butter
grated rind of 2 oranges
2 eggs, separated

2 tbsp. orange-flavored liqueur or rum
1 tbsp. freshly squeezed orange juice
confectioners' sugar, for dusting
1 orange, chopped, to decorate

1 Bring the milk to a boil in a large saucepan over medium-high heat. Add the salt and vanilla bean and seeds, and sprinkle in the rice. Return to a boil, stirring once or twice. Reduce the heat and simmer, stirring frequently, for about 10 minutes.

2 Add the sugar and butter and continue to simmer for about 10 minutes, stirring frequently, until thick and creamy. Pour into a bowl and stir in the orange rind; remove the vanilla bean. Cool to room temperature, stirring occasionally.

3 Beat the egg yolks with the liqueur and orange juice, then beat into the cooled rice mixture.

4 Beat the egg whites until they hold their peaks almost stiff but not too dry. Stir a spoonful into the rice mixture to lighten it, then gently fold in the remaining whites.

5 Spoon the mixture into 1/4-cup muffin pan cups, lined with paper liners, filling to the brim. Bake in a preheated oven at 375°F for about 20 minutes until golden

and cooked through. Cool on a wire rack for 2 minutes, then remove the muffins from the pan and cool completely. Decorate with chopped orange and dust with confectioners' sugar before serving.

COOK'S TIP

Rinsing the saucepan with water before adding the milk to boil helps prevent the milk from scorching.

New Orleans Fried Rice Cakes

This classic New Orleans breakfast dish is a cross between a doughnut and a fritter.
Serve the cakes hot, sprinkled with sugar, as a snack or with a Southern-style breakfast.

Makes about 12 cakes

INGREDIENTS

¹/₂ cup long-grain white rice
1 egg
2–3 tbsp. sugar

1¹/₂ tsp. baking powder
¹/₂ tsp. ground cinnamon
¹/₄ tsp. salt
2 tsp. vanilla extract

9 tbsp. all-purpose flour
vegetable oil, for frying
confectioners' sugar, for dusting

1 Bring a saucepan of water to a boil. Sprinkle in the rice and return to a boil, stirring once or twice. Reduce the heat and simmer for 15–20 minutes until the rice is tender. Drain, rinse, and drain again. Spread the rice onto a dry dish towel to dry completely.

2 Using an electric mixer, beat the egg for about 2 minutes until light and frothy. Add the sugar, baking powder, cinnamon, and salt and continue beating until well blended; beat in the vanilla. Add the flour and stir until well blended, then gently fold in the rice. Cover the bowl with plastic wrap and let rest at room temperature for about 20 minutes.

3 Meanwhile, heat about 4 inches of oil in a deep-fat fryer to 190°F, or until a cube of bread browns in about 25–30 seconds.

4 Drop rounded tablespoons of the batter into the oil, about 3 or 4 at a time. Cook for 4–5 minutes, turning gently, until puffed and golden and cooked through.

5 Using a slotted spoon, transfer to double-thickness paper towels to drain. Continue with the remaining batter; keep warm in a low oven while frying the rest. Dust the rice cakes with confectioners' sugar to serve.

Italian Lemon Rice Cake

This lemony cake should have a crisp crust with a soft moist center.
Soaking the currants in rum brings out their fruitiness.

Serves 8–10

INGREDIENTS

4 cups milk
pinch of salt
1 cup arborio or pudding rice
1 vanilla bean, split, seeds removed
  and reserved
¼ cup currants (the European berry,
  not the tiny dried grape)

¼ cup rum or water
2 tsp. melted butter, for greasing
cornmeal or polenta, for dusting
¾ cup sugar
grated rind of 1 large lemon
4 tbsp. butter, diced
3 eggs

2–3 tbsp. lemon juice (optional)
confectioners' sugar

TO SERVE:
6 oz. mascarpone
2 tbsp. rum
2 tbsp. whipping cream

1 Bring the milk to a boil in a heavy-based saucepan. Sprinkle in the salt and rice and bring back to a boil. Add the vanilla bean and seeds to the milk. Reduce the heat and simmer, partially covered, for about 30 minutes, until the rice is tender and the milk is absorbed; stir occasionally.

2 Meanwhile, bring the currants and rum to a boil in a small saucepan; set aside until the rum is absorbed.

3 Brush with butter the bottom and side of a 10-inch cake pan with a removable bottom. Dust with 2–3 tablespoons of cornmeal to coat evenly; shake out any excess.

4 Remove the rice from the heat and remove the vanilla bean. Stir in all but 1 tablespoon of sugar, with the lemon rind and butter, until the sugar is dissolved. Place in iced water to cool; stir in the soaked currants and remaining rum.

5 Using an electric mixer, beat the eggs for about 2 minutes until light and foamy. Gradually beat in about half the rice mixture, then stir in the rest. If using, stir in the lemon juice.

6 Pour into the prepared pan and smooth the top evenly. Sprinkle with the reserved tablespoon of sugar and bake in a preheated oven at 160°F for about 40 minutes until risen and golden and slightly firm. Cool in the pan on a wire rack.

7 Remove the sides of the pan and dust the top with confectioners' sugar. Transfer the cake to a serving plate. Whisk the mascarpone with the rum and cream and serve with the cake.

Sweet Risotto Cake with Muscat Berries

*Served with your favorite summer berries and a scented mascarpone cream,
this baked sweet risotto makes an unusual dessert.*

Serves 6–8

INGREDIENTS

⅓ cup arborio rice
1½ cups milk
3–4 tbsp. sugar
½ tsp. freshly grated nutmeg
salt
1⅔ cups all-purpose flour
1½ tsp. baking powder
1 tsp. baking soda
1–2 tbsp. superfine sugar
1 egg
¾ cup milk

½ cup sour cream or yogurt
1 tbsp. butter, melted
2 tbsp. honey
½ tsp. almond extract
2 tbsp. toasted slivered almonds
2 tbsp. melted butter, for greasing
confectioners' sugar, for dusting
  (optional)

MUSCAT BERRIES:
1 lb. mixed summer berries, such as
  strawberries (halved), raspberries,
  and blueberries
¼ cup Muscat wine
1–2 tbsp. sugar

MASCARPONE CREAM:
2 tbsp. Muscat wine
1 tbsp. honey
½ tsp. almond extract
1 cup mascarpone

1 Put the rice, milk, sugar, nutmeg, and ½ teaspoon of salt in a heavy-based saucepan. Bring to a boil, reduce the heat slightly and cook, stirring constantly, until the rice is tender and the milk almost absorbed. Cool.

2 Combine the flour, baking powder, baking soda, pinch of salt, and the sugar. In a bowl, beat the egg, milk, sour cream, butter, honey, and almond extract with an electric mixer until smooth. Gradually beat in the rice. Stir in the flour mixture and the almonds.

3 Gently spoon the mixture into a 9–10 inch well-greased cake pan with removable bottom, smoothing the top evenly. Bake in a preheated oven at 325°F for about 20 minutes until golden. Cool in the pan on a wire rack.

4 Put the berries in a bowl, add the sugar and wine. To make the mascarpone cream, stir all the ingredients together and chill.

5 Remove the sides of the pan and slide the cake onto a serving plate. Dust with confectioners' sugar and serve the cake warm with the Muscat berries and mascarpone cream (pipe the cream on top of the cake, if preferred).

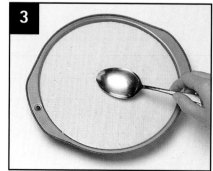

Spicy Carrot-rice Loaf

Rice flour gives this delicious loaf a tender crumb, while the cooked rice adds a chewy texture. Use any kind of cooked rice—long or round, white or brown, even wild.

Serves 8–10

INGREDIENTS

2 cups all-purpose flour
1/2 cup rice flour
2 tsp. baking powder
1/2 tsp. baking soda
1/2 tsp. salt
1 tsp. ground cinnamon
1/2 tsp. freshly ground nutmeg
1/2 tsp. ground ginger

1 cup cooked arborio or long-grain white rice
1/2 cup chopped pecans
1/2 cup golden raisins or raisins
3 eggs
1 cup sugar
1/2 cup lightly packed light brown sugar

8 tbsp. butter, melted and cooled
2 carrots, grated
confectioners' sugar, for dusting

1 Lightly grease a 9 x 5 inch loaf pan. Line with waxed paper and grease; dust lightly with flour.

2 Sift the flour, rice flour, baking powder, baking soda, salt, and spices into a bowl. Add the rice, nuts, and golden raisins and toss well to coat. Make a well in the center of the dry ingredients and set aside.

3 Using an electric mixer, beat the eggs for about 2 minutes until light and foaming. Add the sugars and continue beating for a further 2 minutes. Beat in the melted butter, then stir in the grated carrots until blended.

4 Pour the egg and carrot mixture into the well and, using a fork, stir until a soft batter forms. Do not over mix; the batter should be slightly lumpy.

5 Pour into the prepared pan and smooth the top evenly. Bake in a preheated oven at 350°F for 1–1¼ hours until risen and golden; cover the loaf with foil if it colors too quickly.

6 Cool the loaf in the pan on a wire rack for about 10 minutes. Carefully turn out and let cool completely. Dust with confectioners' sugar and slice thinly to serve.

Index